PEDAL PORTLAND

PEDAL PORTLAND

25 EASY RIDES FOR EXPLORING THE CITY BY BIKE

TODD ROLL

TIMBER PRESS
PORTLAND | LONDON

To my wonderful wife, Lota, my teacher, guide, confidant, and advisor, and to our daughter, Serenne, stalwart ride-tester and quick to tell us when to cut it short. I love you both more than I can express.

Frontispiece: St. Johns Bridge and St. Johns.

Copyright © 2014 by Todd Roll. All rights reserved.
Maps by Lisa Brower of GreenEye Design.
Illustrations by Matt Sundstrom.
Sullivan typeface by Jason Mark Jones.

Published in 2014 by Timber Press, Inc.

The Haseltine Building
133 S.W. Second Avenue,
Suite 450
Portland, Oregon 97204-3527
timberpress.com

6a Lonsdale Road
London NW6 6RD
timberpress.co.uk

Printed in the United States of America

Cover and text design by Laken Wright
Cover illustration by Matt Sundstrom

Library of Congress Cataloging-in-Publication Data

Roll, Todd.
  Pedal Portland: 25 easy rides for exploring the city by bike/
Todd Roll.
     pages cm
  Includes index.
  ISBN 978-1-60469-423-9
1. Cycling—Oregon—Portland—Guidebooks. 2. Portland
(Or.)—Guidebooks. I. Title.
  GV1045.5.O72P678 2014
  796.6'40979549—dc23   2013033880

CONTENTS

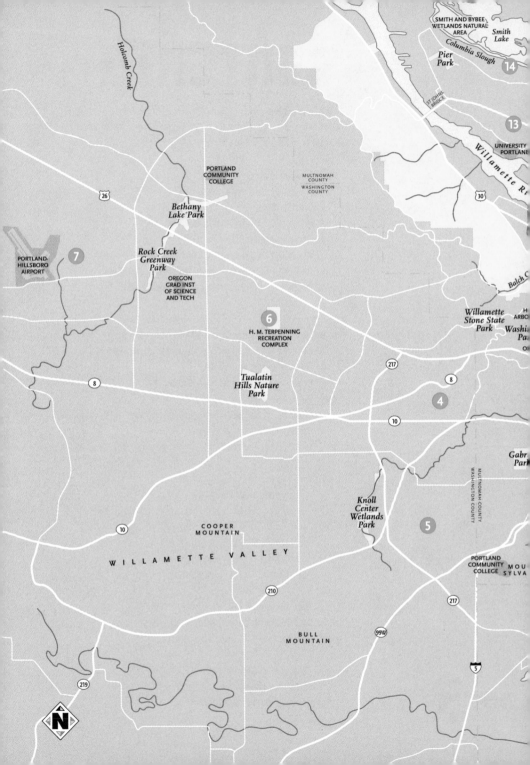

SMITH AND BYBEE
WETLANDS NATURAL
AREA

Smith
Lake

Columbia Slough

Pier
Park

14

ST JOHNS
BRIDGE

13

UNIVERSITY
PORTLAND

Willamette Ri

30

HOLCOMB Creek

26

PORTLAND
COMMUNITY
COLLEGE

MULTNOMAH
COUNTY

WASHINGTON
COUNTY

*Bethany
Lake Park*

PORTLAND-
HILLSBORO
AIRPORT

7

*Rock Creek
Greenway
Park*

OREGON
GRAD INST
OF SCIENCE
AND TECH

6

H. M. TERPENNING
RECREATION
COMPLEX

*Willamette
Stone State
Park*

H
ARBO

Washi
Pa

217

8

4

*Tualatin
Hills Nature
Park*

8

10

10

*Gabr
Par*

*Knoll
Center
Wetlands
Park*

5

MULTNOMAH COUNTY
WASHINGTON COUNTY

COOPER
MOUNTAIN

W I L L A M E T T E   V A L L E Y

PORTLAND
COMMUNITY
COLLEGE

MOU
SYLVA

210

217

BULL
MOUNTAIN

99W

5

219

N

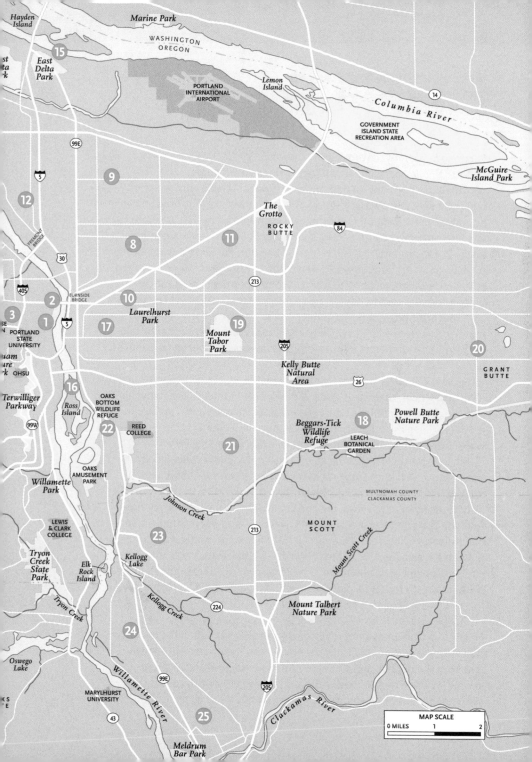

PREFACE

Portland is bicycle nirvana.

The city itself is fascinating (rivers, bridges, lava domes, and more cool than can be counted) and the ever-expanding bike infrastructure makes for safe and pleasant riding. This book's twenty-five rides take full advantage of the beautiful, natural, and even wild areas that are close by, or sometimes directly immersed in, the city hubbub. And the quality of biking in and around Portland is hard to dispute. Portland welcomes city planners from around the world who come to experience what has been achieved here, and in 2008, it was awarded a platinum-level rating for bicycle-friendly community by the League of American Bicyclists. *Bicycling* magazine often ranks Portland number one in their list of most bike-friendly cities in the country. The people, too, are as friendly as the bike infrastructure, and more importantly, the drivers are courteous. What's not to love?

For me, it's pretty simple. No matter where I go, I think about my bike. If I'm on my bike, then life is good. But more often than I'd like, when I'm going to some far corner of the Portland area on an errand, I go by car. It's those times especially that I think about how I could get there on two wheels, and what adventures I might have had along the way.

When it comes to exploring a city, the automobile—while quick, warm, dry, and (I hope) in possession of a good stereo—has a lot of drawbacks. Cars move too quickly to absorb the details; the driver, especially, is likely to miss views, big and small. Roof and glass separate you from the surrounding smells, sounds, weather, and people that are so much a part of the place. Parking can be difficult and costly, and exercise is almost nonexistent. Never mind what great bakeries, parks, or art galleries you might have missed on the way to your destination. Walking is the best way to explore a place up close, but you need many tiring days to see a city of even modest size on foot.

The bicycle is the happy medium. By moving quickly, yet using a relatively low amount of energy, you can go far without taking the next two days off to heal blisters. At the same time, you'll move slowly enough to take in the details, and it couldn't be easier to pull over and look around. With no roof or glass between you and the world, you engage every sense. Sure, rain can be annoying, but not if you have the right waterproof clothes. And when you want to lock your bike and become a pedestrian, the parking is free. And everywhere.

With this book, I hope to wrestle the bicycle back from the pack of red-faced, smooth-legged heroes with gargantuan thighs in skin tight spandex heaving their way across the finish line. With this dominating image has come the idea that if we don't push our limits, compete, sweat, and win, then why bother? The reality is, all you really need to do to maintain good health is just move your body. These tours aren't about maximizing your fitness level, tackling lung-busting hills, or trying to hit all the green lights. Heck, you might not even sweat! But you'll get exercise just by turning the pedals, and more importantly, you'll see Portland up close. Wear your street clothes, pack a rain jacket, pop on a helmet, and go.

The routes are designed to be fun, easy, and safe enough for everyone. Do you have a couple of rusting mountain bikes and a kids' trailer in the garage? That's more than enough. Pick a ride in a part of town you've never been to, or choose to see your own neighborhood from a new perspective. All you need is an afternoon to experience the city like never before. If you don't come away with memories of a brilliantly colored bird, a mini-market with a funny name, a beautiful tree, or a cute cottage with a lovely flower garden, you went too fast.

HOW TO PEDAL PORTLAND

Use this book like a guidebook: look at the overview map, decide on your next adventure, go to that chapter, and get started. Each chapter consists of a route map, helpful stats (distance, elevation, and how to get to the starting point), and turn-by-turn directions. Beyond the turns, you'll learn the history, features, and other fun facts about the things you're riding past.

What to Expect

Before you choose your own adventure, know that these routes were created with a few goals in mind: namely, to keep them accessible, safe, interesting, and fun.

Doable distances, loops, and no big hills

The rides in this book were designed to be accessible to anyone, including children on their own bikes (or in a trailer, tag-a-long, or child's seat) or visually or balance-impaired people on the back of a tandem or on an adult tricycle. The average ride is around 10 miles long. Even if you're not used to biking, 10 miles (or 8 or 12) should be attainable. You may be sore afterward, but there's no shame in that. If this distance is just a warm-up for you, consider linking together rides that are near one another and doubling your mileage.

All but two of the rides in this book are loops. There's something mystical about heading off in one direction and arriving back at the same place from a different direction. Plus, you see twice as much that way. The non-loop rides (see rides 3 and 4) end at different transit points than where they began in order to avoid climbing a big hill. Speaking of which, hills can be a bummer—especially if you're not used to them or are hauling two kids in a trailer—so you won't find many on these routes. Eighteen of the rides have less than 200 feet of elevation gain, the rest have less than 300.

Since these rides are relatively short and flat, almost any bike should work. The single-speed beach cruiser may be the exception, but even that should be okay for all but the occasional steep hill. (If you need to rent a bike, see page 204 for Portland-area bike shops that offer rentals.) All rides were tested using "Pee Wee Herman 2"—my eight-speed, 37-pound city hybrid bike. It has just enough gears, a basket, a rack to carry treasures, and a nice comfortable upright riding position so I can see cars and they can see me. A handlebar bag with a map pocket on top works great to keep the route map just a glance away.

The quietest roads possible

As of 2013, Portland could boast more than 300 miles of bikeways: 79 miles of multi-use paths, 59 miles of neighborhood greenways, and 181 miles of bike lanes. The numbers are expected to keep growing, and the routes in this book explore many of these excellent streets and paths, avoiding busy car-filled streets whenever possible.

- **Multi-use paths.** These car-free paths (the Springwater Corridor Trail, for example) are by far the safest place to ride and often go through beautiful natural areas. Their only drawback is they can isolate you from the surrounding neighborhood.
- **Neighborhood greenways.** Formerly known as bicycle boulevards, these are the quietest and safest routes for bikes beyond multi-use paths. The city has improved this network of naturally low-traffic streets, making them even more bike friendly, by installing time and distance signage, speed bumps, traffic circles, and even concrete barriers with openings only for bikes. You know you're biking on a neighborhood greenway when you see a sharrow—pavement markings of a white bicycle with two arrows above it.

Fun for everyone

These scenic and historic routes are designed to be enjoyed by everyone, including kids. Since youngsters aren't always fascinated by the same things us old folks are, at the beginning of each ride are a few scavenger hunt items for young riders and passengers to look for along the route. Can you find them all? An answer key appears on page 206.

Navigating Portland

Getting around Portland is pretty easy if you know a few basics. Burnside Street divides north and south and the Willamette River divides east and west. This makes four quadrants: NW, NE, SE, SW. To complicate things just slightly, a fifth "quadrant"—North Portland (N)—consists of the peninsula between the Willamette and Columbia rivers, west of N Williams. North-south avenues are generally numbered, getting higher as you move in either direction away from the Willamette River; west-east streets are named.

Bike maps are available that cover every part of the metropolitan area, including each of the city's quadrants, several of the larger area cities, each of the counties, and one of the whole metro area. Find them at bike shops, the Pioneer Courthouse Square Visitor's Center, the PDX Welcome Center at Portland International Airport, and through the City of Portland's website (portlandonline.com).

Transit

Sometimes it may be faster to simply bike to the ride's starting point, but especially for trips longer than five miles, using Portland's public transportation system (TriMet; trimet.org) is a great option. All forms of transit are bike friendly: just pay your fare and your bike rides for free! Here are the ways to get where you want to go:

MAX (Metropolitan Area Express) light rail has four lines: red, blue, yellow, and green (a fifth, the orange line, is expected to begin service in 2015). MAX runs fairly frequently (usually every

15 minutes or better) connecting the edges of the city to the center. Hang your bike by its front tire on the hooks inside the car doors. There are usually two cars; use the one with ground-level entry rather than stairs.

THE PORTLAND STREETCAR is similar to MAX except its cars are shorter and lighter, and it runs on its own set of tracks on two lines. The North South Line (NS) runs from Nob Hill in Northwest Portland to the South Waterfront. The Central Loop Line (CL) runs across the river via the Broadway Bridge, and, beginning in 2015, on the Portland-Milwaukie Light Rail Bridge to the South Waterfront. The system for bringing bikes aboard the Portland Streetcar is the same as on MAX.

TRIMET BUSES may not be as flashy or beloved as the Portland Street-car or MAX, but with more than 600 buses on around 80 routes, they can get you almost anywhere in the city. To plan how to combine your ride with the bus, call 503.238.RIDE (7433). All TriMet buses have a front rack that holds two bikes. To use, fold the rack down and place the rack's spring-loaded arm on the top of your front wheel to hold your bike in the rack. Always make eye contact with the driver and indicate that you are going to load your bike; when getting off the bus, exit through the front door and tell the driver that you want to take your bike off.

WES (Westside Express Service) is a commuter rail line running almost 15 miles from Beaverton to Wilsonville. This full-sized train line stops at five stations on the original Oregon Electric Railway which stopped passenger service in 1933.

Staying Safe

By law you are a moving vehicle and must ride like one. Follow these rules of the road:

- **Be visible.** Ride where drivers can see you and make eye contact with motorists to let them know you're there. Wear brightly colored clothing at all times. At night, by law, you must use a white front light and red rear reflector. Using a red rear light is even smarter.
- **Signal smart.** Use hand and arm signals (as long as you can do so safely) to indicate your intention to stop, merge, or turn.

- **Be predictable.** Ride with traffic, and obey all stop signs, lights, and lane markings. Ride in a straight line and don't swerve between parked cars. Stay to the right unless you're making a left turn. Check your blind spot before turning.
- **Pass with care.** Audibly signal your intention to pass, either with a bell or by voice—"on your left" works great. Don't pass bikes (or cars) on the right.
- **Yield to pedestrians.** Give pedestrians the right of way at all intersections, whether they have a painted crosswalk or not.
- **Avoid riding on the sidewalk.** It's against the law to ride on the sidewalk in downtown Portland—between SW Jefferson, Naito Parkway, NW Hoyt, and 13th Avenue—and the offense carries a $500 fine. I tend to follow this rule everywhere unless the street is particularly dangerous and pedestrians are very few. If you have to do it, ride slowly, yield to pedestrians, and watch for cars, especially when coming off the sidewalk.
- **Anticipate conflicts.** Stay aware of traffic around you and be prepared to react. Stay extra alert at intersections and watch out for the right hook: a car making a right turn in front of you without seeing you. Riding slowly is an incredibly effective way to stay out of trouble.
- **Wear a helmet.** Oregon law requires that all children under age sixteen wear a helmet when biking, but they are recommended for everyone. Helmets are required for everyone in Washington. Make

RIGHT

ALTERNATIVE
RIGHT

sure that the helmet fits snugly on top of your head, not tipped back-
ward or forward. After a crash or any impact that affects your helmet,
visible or not, replace it immediately.

- **Cross carefully.** Always cross railroad, streetcar, and MAX tracks at a
  90 degree angle so your front tire doesn't get caught in the groove and
  send you flying over the handlebars.

- **Prepare for rain.** It is Portland, after all. Biking safely in the rain simply means to go slower, brake earlier, and avoid riding over metal
  (like manhole covers), especially when turning or braking. You'll stay
  cleaner and drier if your bike has fenders and if you have a few basic
  items of rain gear.

Keeping your bike safe

Bike theft does happen, but you can help prevent it by following a few
simple rules. Use a U-lock instead of a cable lock, which can be easily cut. Lock your bike, both frame and wheel, to a solid metal object. A
bike rack is the obvious first choice, but a parking meter or metal sign
post are good alternatives. The citywide standard bike rack is called a
staple rack because of its shape; you'll find bike corrals (multiple staple
racks grouped together) all around the city. Never leave your bike outside overnight. For added protection, remove your front wheel and lock
it too. Remove the saddle and seat post if you're really worried.

PORTLAND'S BIKE INFRASTRUCTURE

BIKE BOXES. These green boxes, painted on the street at busy intersections, help cyclists be seen by cars and reduce the incidence of right-hook collisions. If the light is green, bike through the intersection as you normally would. At a red light, move into the green box so cars can easily see you. When the light turns green, go through the intersection first.

COPENHAGEN LEFT. This is a box painted on the ground at a light that prominently shows cars that you want to turn left. If you want to turn left, put your bike into the box and go through the intersection according to normal traffic laws.

CYCLE TRACK. This is a glorified bike lane borrowed from Europe. It is a wide bike lane next to the sidewalk with parked cars forming a natural protection from moving traffic. In between the parked cars and the bike lane is a 3-foot-wide "shy zone" that helps eliminate the possibility of a car door suddenly being opened right in your path, in other words being "doored."

Biking Portland: Then and Now

Bicycling in Portland dates back to at least the 1880s when daredevil high-wheeled bicycle rider Fred T. Merrill moved to town, attracted by reports of a rival stunt rider. After Merrill shamed his nemesis out of town with his daring feats high above the ground on the ungainly machine, he stuck around until the safety bicycle—basically what we know today—arrived on the scene. Later he boasted of selling 52,000 bikes in 20 years. It wasn't too long after that, 1896, when Portland's first bike map was created, sponsored by the Multnomah Wheelmen Bike Club. The cartographer for Metro's updated regional bike map, *Bike There!*, used it as inspiration. The main difference just might be the lack of taverns on the current map.

In 1971, Oregon passed the Bicycle Bill, the first law in the country mandating that 1 percent of highway funds be used to build bike and pedestrian infrastructure. However, a lack of specifics on how to implement the law meant that money didn't get allocated until the mid-1990s when the Bicycle Transportation Alliance, a local advocacy group, sued the City of Portland for not including bike lanes in a road project.

In 1994, a few local activists created the Yellow Bike Project, which put nearly 400 mustard-yellow bikes on the streets for people to use at no charge. They began by asking the Community Cycling Center, a bike-oriented nonprofit, to donate ten broken-down clunkers. They fixed up the bikes, painted them a distinctive yellow color, and affixed a sign reading "free community bike, use at own risk" and a phone number to call for repair. Great press coverage spurred more donations and soon fifty more yellow bikes hit the street. The program eventually received national attention and the city donated warehouse space to the program. Unfortunately the inevitable happened: the bikes all got vandalized or stolen. But the program did inspire other communities around the country to try their own bike-share programs. Now bike share is coming back in a big way: a credit card–based system with about 750 bikes stationed at 75 kiosks in Portland's inner city is due to launch. None of the bikes will be yellow.

Passed in 2010, The Portland Bicycle Plan for 2030 envisions bicycling as a "fundamental pillar of Portland's fully integrated transportation system." One of the plan's ambitious goals is to double the city's bikeways to 630 miles by 2016, and 962 miles by 2030. Another is to increase the number of bike commuters to 25 percent from 6.3 percent in 2013 (already a 238 percent increase since 2000). Not included in the plan, but bound to happen anyway, is the continued proliferation of bike-focused events—Pedalpalooza, Sunday Parkways, and the World Naked Bike Ride, to name a few—that help keep Portland fun and weird.

All of this infrastructure adds up to some serious bike fun. Pair safe biking streets with courteous drivers and scads of great neighborhoods and you've got a lifetime of exploring to do. So what are you waiting for? We'll see you out on the road!

1 HISTORIC CITY CENTER

SCAVENGER HUNT

A fence made of railroad tracks

. . . .

A "pile" of kids bikes where Zoobombers meet

. . . .

An 18-foot-tall statue entitled *Theodore Roosevelt—Rough Rider*

. . . .

THIS ESSENTIAL RIDE through downtown Portland begins at Skidmore Fountain, funded in part by pharmacist Steven Skidmore, so that "horses, men and dogs" could find refreshment. At the fountain's 1888 dedication, Portland brewer Henry Weinhard offered to pump beer from his brewery through it. From the fountain, the route winds past the elegant 1890s cast-iron-fronted buildings of Old Town and Chinatown, delves into the shabby-turned-chic streets of the Pearl District, rolls up a gentle hill lined with art and architecture to Oregon's largest university, and zips down to the green beauty and soaring views on both sides of the river before returning to the site of the wild party that never was (alas, the city turned Weinhard down).

Ride on a Saturday mid-March through December and you can also check out two iconic Portland shopping experiences: the Portland Saturday Market featuring handmade crafts near the start, and the Portland Farmers Market in the South Park Blocks. At any time of the year or day, you'll find a plethora of refreshment options along this city ride. After 137 years, however, Henry Weinhard's brewery in the Pearl District is no longer in operation.

STARTING POINT
Skidmore Fountain MAX station (1st Avenue under the Burnside Bridge)

8.32
miles

DISTANCE

MODERATE
226 feet

DIFFICULTY & ELEVATION GAIN

TRANSIT AND PARKING

TriMet's MAX Red and Blue lines stop at the Skidmore Fountain station. TriMet buses 12, 19, and 20 stop at SW 2nd and W Burnside, and several other lines stop at the bus mall on SW 5th and SW 6th. Look for street parking with long enough meter time or park in any of the numerous pay lots.

TANNER SPRINGS PARK

0.0 mi. Begin at the Skidmore Fountain MAX station and walk your bike south on 1st, away from the Burnside Bridge.

0.07 mi. Right on SW Ash. At the corner of Ash and SW 3rd, glance to your right: an out-the-door line at Voodoo Doughnuts ① is practically a guaranteed sight.

0.17 mi. Left on SW 3rd.

0.22 mi. Left on SW Pine.

0.37 mi. Cross SW Naito, enter Governor Tom McCall Waterfront Park, and turn left on the waterfront path. This popular bike and pedestrian path occupies the former site of the six-lane Harbor Drive. The park's name honors Oregon's governor in the late 1960s and 1970s, Tom McCall, who authorized removing the freeway and replacing it with this green space, a novel concept.

0.68 mi. Pass under the Burnside Bridge. Turn left at the large boulders in the middle of the Japanese American Historical Plaza ②. Exit the park, crossing NW Naito on NW Couch.

0.82 mi. From Couch, turn right on NW 2nd.

0.97 mi. Left on NW Flanders and left on NW 3rd. The white walls of the Lan Su Chinese Garden are studded with 40 "leak" windows that offer peeks into the garden. Each window has a graceful nature-themed pattern but no two are the same.

1.09 mi. Right on NW Davis. The North Park Blocks, laid out in the 1860s, greet you between NW 8th and NW Park as you ride west, dividing Old Town Chinatown and the Pearl District. This leafy oasis is mirrored by the South Park Blocks on the other end of downtown. It was originally intended to be a continuous uninterrupted linear park with the property to be donated by each

①

Feeling peckish or sluggish at the beginning of the ride—or absolutely sugar starved at the end? Consider a detour to Voodoo Doughnuts (22 SW 3rd), elevated to a must-try stop for visitors after exposure on television shows like *Rachel Ray*, *Top Chef*, and *Man v. Food*. The locals like it pretty well too. The line can take more than an hour, but the reward—a bright pink box full of sugar bombs like the bacon maple bar, the Captain my Captain (with Captain Crunch sprinkles) or the Memphis Mafia (a banana, chocolate, peanut butter concoction)—is worth the wait. And what would a doughnut be without coffee? Portland's most famous roaster, Stumptown Coffee (128 SW 3rd), fuses passion for high-quality, fair-trade coffee with a style that captures the spirit of the Northwest.

ROSE QUARTER

NW MARSHALL ST

Tanner Springs Park

NW LOVEJOY ST ③

NW JOHNSON ST

Couch Park

NW HOYT ST

UNION STATION

NW GLISAN ST

NW FLANDERS ST

North Park Blocks

NW DAVIS ST

NW COUCH ST

W BURNSIDE ST

STEEL BRIDGE

BURNSIDE BRIDGE

JELD-WEN FIELD

SW WASHINGTON ST

SW ALDER ST

SW STARK ST

SW PINE ST ①

SW ASH ST ②

Waterfront Park

Willamette River

SW MORRISON ST

SW MAIN ST

SW COLUMBIA ST

SW BROADWAY ④

SW SALMON ST

MORRISON BRIDGE

SW MADISON ST

99W

SW JEFFERSON ST

SALMON ST SPRINGS

Vera Katz Eastbank Esplanade

SW CLAY ST

SW MARKET ST

South Park Blocks

PORTLAND STATE UNIVERSITY

Ira Keller Fountain Park

HAWTHORNE BRIDGE

Governor Tom McCall Waterfront Park

⑤

SE WATER AVE

SW HARRISON ST

South Park Blocks

SW HALL ST

Pettygrove Park

HARBOR DR

HARBOR WY

MONTGOMERY ST

South Waterfront Park

Lovejoy Fountain Park

RIVER DR

Governors Park

N

Duniway Park

RIVER PKWY

MARQUAM BRIDGE

MAP SCALE
0 MILES   1/8   1/4

MAP KEY

— ROUTE
⋯ NEIGHBORHOOD GREENWAYS
- - CAR FREE TRAIL
▢ PARK/GREENSPACE
▪ LANDMARKS

ROUTE ELEVATION

ELEVATION (feet)

300
200
100
0

0 MILES   1.7   3.3   5   6.7   8.32

landowner. But several blocks south of Burnside were never donated, resulting in the two separated parks we have today.

1.43 mi. Right on NW 9th. Here, you're just a few blocks away from Powell's City of Books (1005 W Burnside)—a local landmark that boasts more than a million new and used titles under its roof. If you visit, beware: what many intend as a quick stroll through the color-coded rooms can easily slip into an afternoon-long affair. At 9th and NW Irving is the Ecotrust building, an 1896 shipping warehouse turned into a complex of eco-friendly non-profits and delicious local eateries.

1.88 mi. From 9th, turn left on NW Marshall. Naturalistic Tanner Springs Park ❸ is at 10th. At the corner of 16th and Marshall is the seedy-looking bar Slabtown. In the 1880s, this was also the name for the neighborhood, whose low-income residents would get the unwanted rounded outside slabs of wood from nearby mills.

2.5 mi. Left on NW 20th.

2.75 mi. Left on NW Hoyt. At the corner of 20th and Hoyt is the castle-like William Temple House. Built in 1892 by physician K.A.J. Mackenzie, today it serves as headquarters for the Oregon Episcopal Church's counseling center.

2.96 mi. Left on NW 17th.

3.05 mi. Right on NW Johnson.

3.25 mi. Right on NW 13th.

3.66 mi. Left on SW Stark.

Along the waterfront path, just north of the Burnside Bridge, the 100 ornamental cherry trees are part of the Japanese American Historical Plaza. Memorials engraved into boulders tell the story of the Japanese Americans who were deported to internment camps in eastern Washington, Idaho, and California at the beginning of World War II. Brass plaques bearing the official apology from President Ronald Reagan and the Bill of Rights serve as reminders of the dangers of stereotyping groups at the expense of individuals' rights.

Tanner Springs Park is a modern version of the original lake and wetland that were drained to make space for industry. Today, city water bubbles between the benches, runs downhill and into the pond at the bottom of the park where it evaporates or is absorbed naturally into the ground. This natural park is filled with native wetland plants that attract frequent visitors like ducks, dragonflies, and hummingbirds are frequent visitors. The grassy benches are great places to contemplate the natural and built environment, including a fence built from old railroad tracks.

3.87 mi. Right on SW 9th. Ready for a snack? Or to make an absolute raving pig of yourself? You're in luck: one block ahead, the food cart pod at SW Washington is among Portland's largest and most diversely scrumptious.

4.16 mi. After crossing SW Salmon, 9th becomes SW Park and you enter the South Park Blocks and Cultural District ④. Continue biking south, passing several historical landmarks as well as the site of the Portland Farmers Market (between SW Hall and SW Montgomery) where crowds of discerning locavores, including celebrity chefs, ply the circuit: eyeing, sniffing, tasting, and collecting fresh produce, meat, eggs, artisan bread, wine, cheese, beer, cider, jam, and more.

4.63 mi. Left on unmarked SW Harrison. After crossing SW Harbor, Harrison becomes SW Moody/River Parkway.

5.44 mi. Turn left at the crosswalk across from the Marriott Hotel, left on the waterfront path, and left again when the path reaches the river.

5.65 mi. Turn left on SW Montgomery at the roundabout with a tree in the center. The inviting stretch in front of the McCormick and Schmick's restaurant, and its resident brewery Full Sail, is often crowded in summertime. Every December, the gaily lit boats of the Christmas Ship Parade stop in the harbor here and give diners a front row view.

5.78 mi. Right on SW Harbor.

5.91 mi. Left on the path to reenter Governor Tom McCall Waterfront Park.

6.05 mi. Turn left onto the narrow path that curves right and leads onto the Hawthorne Bridge. Ride across.

6.45 mi. After crossing the river, turn right to descend the ramp—be prepared to stop at the bottom—and turn right onto the Vera Katz Eastbank Esplanade ❺. On the stretch of the esplanade starting at the Morrison Bridge, look for four sculptures that evoke the history of the river. The first is Echo Gate (go ahead and ride through). Situated in the loudest place on the esplanade, it looks like an ear listening to deafening decibels of the freeway. Next are Ghost Ship and Stack Stalk at opposite ends of a pier that once stood here, and finally Alluvial Wall, which shows the flowing river bottom as well as the human elements (trash) found in waterways near where humans live.

The Cultural District (noted by the street-sign toppers and bound by Market and Salmon to the north and south, and Broadway and 10th from east to west) is home to the Portland Art Museum, the Arlene Schnitzer Concert Hall, the New Theatre, and the Oregon Historical Society, as well as two pre-1900 churches: the 1895 First Congregational Church with its beautiful stained glass windows, and the looming Gothic 1889 St. James Lutheran Church (at Jefferson and Park). Sadly for art lovers of a different stripe, there's nary a tattoo parlor in sight.

The ride south on SW Park is dotted with historical landmarks. At SW Jefferson is a stone memorial to the Great Plank Road. On this road, farmers could transport their products from the fertile valley over the west hills to the deep water port of Portland. This allowed Portland, and not one of the other nearby muddy riverside clearings in the forest, to become the local powerhouse. At SW Market is Lincoln Hall, originally a high school and the first building on the campus of Portland State University. At SW Montgomery is the Simon Benson House, which once belonged to Oregon's most generous lumber baron. Stop for a drink of water from the Benson Bubbler in front of the house. This is one of the twenty original fountains Benson donated to the city in 1912, and the model for public fountains all over Portland.

7.2 mi. Turn left at the Ash St. sign and go down the ramp onto the 1200-foot-long floating walkway—the longest in the United States. Fixed to pylons, it rises and falls with changing river levels that can fluctuate seasonally up to 35 feet or more (the walkway closed in June 2011 due to high water). Stop on the walkway to admire the Steel Bridge and feel the water move beneath you.

7.7 mi. Stay on the path as it veers left and crosses the Steel Bridge. Turn left at the end of the bridge and continue on the waterfront path.

8.21 mi. Just past the Burnside Bridge on your right is the site of the Portland Saturday Market. Turn right here and cross SW Naito.

8.32 mi. Back to the start.

The Vera Katz Eastbank Esplanade is the pride and joy of waterfront biking with its sweeping views of the city skyline (try to ignore the roar of cars on I-5 next to you). Once part of the City of East Portland, much of the eastern bank of the Willamette was wetland, unsuitable for the kind of warehouses and industry that made the west bank such an economic powerhouse. However, its location across from the bustling town of Portland was too desirable to leave fallow. Before long, entrepreneurs had built long piers out to water deep enough for the sailing ships of the day. Gradually the wetlands were filled in with sawdust, garbage, and construction debris (concrete trucks would back right up to the river and dump excess concrete).

In 1998, then-mayor Vera Katz authorized constructing a bike path while at the same time restoring the banks of the river to a more natural state. The plans included planting 280 trees and 43,695 shrubs. Completed after two and a half years of construction, the Eastbank Esplanade runs for 1.5 miles between the Steel and Hawthorne bridges. A bronze statue of Vera Katz lounges on a concrete bench just past the fire station, keeping an eye on her pride and joy (and on the homeless camp under the bridge).

2 FIVE BRIDGES

WITH 13 BRIDGES that span more than a century, Portland is a bridge lover's dream. One of them is one-of-a-kind, another is the oldest of its type in the country. Of the two that carry thousands of cars a day, one is elegant as a result of the public outcry about the ugliness of the other. Each bridge is unique, offering views of the city from different perspectives.

To ride across a bridge on a bike is a vastly more stimulating experience than inside the glass and metal cocoon of an automobile. Biking allows you to cross slowly enough to notice the interesting structure, enjoy the views and refreshing smell of the river, and feel the wind in your face. This curvy ride takes you over five of the city's most beautiful downtown bridges—and within sight of two more. In the process you'll learn about the differences between them and the neighborhoods they connect.

SCAVENGER HUNT

A polished granite model of the Willamette River in the sidewalk

Statues of snails: What do you think their "heads" look like?

A pair of 20-foot-tall stainless steel sculptures that play music

STARTING POINT
Skidmore Fountain MAX
station (1st Avenue under
the Burnside Bridge)

7.53
miles

DISTANCE

EASY
171 feet

DIFFICULTY &
ELEVATION GAIN

TRANSIT AND PARKING

TriMet's MAX Red and Blue lines stop at the Skidmore Fountain station. TriMet buses 12, 19, and 20 stop at SW 2nd and W Burnside, and several other lines stop at the bus mall on SW 5th and SW 6th. If you drove, look for street parking spots with long enough meter time or park in any of the numerous pay lots.

THE STEEL BRIDGE

0.0 mi. Begin at the Skidmore Fountain MAX station and walk your bike south on 1st, away from the Burnside Bridge.

0.07 mi. Right on SW Ash and right on SW 2nd.

0.08 mi. Right on W Burnside and cross the bridge. The 1926 Burnside Bridge, unique in many ways, is also the only bridge on this route with a street-level bike lane rather than a separated raised bike and walkway. This double-leaf bascule bridge, or drawbridge, uses counterweights to help lift the two decks up—a very energy efficient system. The ornate towers with red tile roofs were designed with the help of an architect to enhance the bridge's artistic value. From the middle of the Burnside Bridge, you can see several other bridges in each direction, as well as the Portland, Oregon, sign with a leaping stag and the outline of the state.

0.59 mi. At SE Martin Luther King Jr. Blvd, turn right on the sidewalk and walk your bike for the next block to avoid the right lane streetcar tracks. Remount and turn right at SE Ankeny for a block of cobblestone biking.

0.74 mi. Right on SE 2nd. Check out the legendary Burnside Skatepark ❶ underneath the bridge. Return the way you came on 2nd and continue south toward Stark.

0.97 mi. Right on SE Stark. The name changes to SE Water after bending to the left.

❶ Underneath the Burnside Bridge at its east end is the Burnside Skatepark, a successful example, in a sport that prides itself on being counterculture, of building something completely illegally and in the process, sticking it to the man and changing the face of public recreation. In 1990, back when the thought of a skateboard park made mayors cringe and lawyers chuckle, a bunch of kids took the bags of concrete they were going to use to build a ramp in their backyard (before the landlord found out) and decided to make a ramp against the wall under the Burnside Bridge. The spot wasn't ideal—next to the railroad tracks and full of syringes, dirty mattresses, soiled clothes, and sketchy lurkers—but it was dry. They made their ramp, then another, and it was good. Then the I-84 onramp got built and a deal was cut with the concrete trucks to drop off their leftovers, and things got sick, that is, real good. Pro skaters regularly came from around the world to try their skills at a park built by skaters, for skaters. Today, skateboard parks are everywhere and Burnside's place in history is secured.

Willamette River

The Fields Neighborhood Park

NW NAITO PKWY

N LARRABEE AVE

99W

NE BROADWAY

NE WEIDLER ST

NW OVERTON ST

NW NORTHRUP ST

NW MARSHALL ST

4

Tanner Springs Park

NW STATION WY

BROADWAY BRIDGE

5

ROSE QUARTER

NE GRAND AVE

NE MULTNOMAH ST

NW LOVEJOY ST

N INTERSTATE AVE

UNION STATION

NE HOLLADAY ST

NW 11TH AVE

NW 10TH AVE

NW 9TH AVE

NW IRVING ST

NE OREGON ST

OREGON CONVENTION CENTER

NW 14TH AVE

405

NW GLISAN ST

NW 6TH AVE

NW BROADWAY

3

STEEL BRIDGE

NE LLOYD BLVD

30

NW EVERETT ST

84

North Park Blocks

NW 2ND AVE

NW 1ST AVE

NW COUCH ST

NW Couch ST

W BURNSIDE ST

E BURNSIDE ST

SW ANKENY ST

ASH ST

BURNSIDE BRIDGE

1

SE ANKENY ST

SW OAK ST

SW STARK ST

SW PINE ST

Waterfront Park

SW WASHINGTON ST

SW ALDER ST

SW 7TH AVE

SW 5TH AVE

SW 4TH AVE

SW 3RD AVE

5

SE 3RD AVE

MARTIN LUTHER KING JR BLVD

SE STARK ST

SW TAYLOR ST

SW SALMON ST

SW MAIN ST

SW MORRISON ST

SW YAMHILL ST

MORRISON BRIDGE

SE 2ND AVE

SE MORRISON ST

SW 12TH AVE

SW BROADWAY

SW 6TH AVE

SW 2ND AVE

SW 1ST AVE

99W

2

SE BELMONT ST

SE YAMHILL ST

SW CLAY ST

SW MARKET ST

South Park Blocks

SW MADISON ST

SW JEFFERSON ST

SW COLUMBIA ST

Vera Katz Eastbank Esplanade

SE WATER AVE

99E

SE GRAND AVE

SE 7TH AVE

PORTLAND STATE UNIVERSITY

SW NAITO PKWY

HAWTHORNE BRIDGE

SE MADISON ST

SE HAWTHORNE ST

SE CLAY ST

N

SW HARRISON ST

South Waterfront Park

MAP SCALE

0 MILES   1/8   1/4

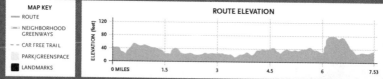

ROUTE ELEVATION

ELEVATION (feet)

120

80

40

0

0 MILES   1.5   3   4.5   6   7.53

1.38 mi. Pass under the Morrison Bridge ❷ and turn right on the two-way bike ramp that leads up onto the bridge. (It's easy to miss the bike ramp entrance: if you hit SW Yamhill, you went a few yards too far. Backtrack, or take the opportunity to explore this former industrial area). Ride across on the 15-foot-wide path for bikes and pedestrians.

1.85 mi. Stay left to get off the bridge after crossing the river. Wind down the ramp, cross SW Naito at the crosswalk, and turn right on the path into Governor Tom McCall Waterfront Park.

2.19 mi. The next bridge you'll pass under is the Hawthorne. Turn right at the large concrete planter and go up the small incline and narrow path (follow the bike sign "SE Portland") onto the Hawthorne Bridge. Built in 1910, this is the oldest vertical lift bridge in the United States. A 1999 restoration widened the sidewalks to ten feet to encourage commuters. It worked: the bridge carries more than 8000 bikers a day. The Marquam Bridge to your right was built on a budget—it cost only $14 million—but offended the public greatly and prompted a formal protest from the Portland Arts Commission. Former Mayor Vera Katz called it "a Berlin wall dividing east and west."

2.63 mi. Look for a ramp on your right to exit the bridge after crossing the river (follow the bike sign "Eastbank Esplanade"). Wind slowly down the ramp and turn right at the bottom. As you bike along the esplanade, look for interpretive signs revealing the history of the waterfront at the foot of each intersecting street.

3.38 mi. Still on the esplanade, turn left at the Ash St. sign and go down the ramp onto the floating walkway.

3.9 mi. Turn left onto the Steel Bridge ❸ and ride slowly across on its narrow pathway. This is the lowest of the

❷

The current Morrison Bridge is a bascule bridge (like the Burnside and the Broadway) and is the third bridge in this spot. The 1887 original, Portland's first bridge, was a toll bridge that charged 5 cents for a pedestrian to cross. That bridge was replaced in 1905, and again in 1958. The first ten to fifteen blocks on the east side of the river are the Central Eastside Industrial District where historically many fruit and vegetable distribution warehouses stood. Today, industrial businesses are still holding out, while the relatively low land prices and chic look of the area's warehouses attract edgy restaurants and the newest of Oregon's liquid obsessions—several artisan liquor distilleries have sprung up in an area now called Distillery Row.

The 1912 Steel Bridge is truly one-of-a-kind thanks to its dual vertical lift decks which move independently of one another. It's also among the world's most multimodal bridges. Besides carrying bikes and pedestrians, it hosts freight and passenger rail, MAX, the streetcar, city buses, and cars. Since the bridge is owned by the railroad, the city was only given a 24-hour permit to install the pedestrian and bicycle deck in 2001. To make sure they could complete the entire project by the deadline, engineers assembled every piece of the deck off site to insure proper fit, and made adjustments before shutting the bridge down and installing the walkway. It worked perfectly.

bridges; if you're lucky a train will be crossing right next to you or rumbling overhead.

4.1 mi. Turn right at the end of the bridge (at the concrete roundabout with the stainless steel sculpture). Turn right again to cross the railroad tracks and then take another right on the private-looking (but wonderfully public) river path.

4.5 mi. The picnic tables as you approach the rusty red Broadway Bridge are a nice place to sit and admire the view. The large grey cylinders across the river are grain elevators, built in 1914, for storing grain shipped to Portland before it is transferred to ocean-going ships and transported around the world. Oregon exports the largest volume of wheat in the United States from this elevator and others like it along the Willamette and Columbia rivers.

4.61 mi. After crossing under the Broadway Bridge, turn left to go down the ramp next to the Albers Mill Building and then take a sharp right to stay on the river path. Built in 1909, the Albers Mill Building operated as a flour mill into the 1980s. The mill's explosions, fires, grain dust, and vermin were such a nuisance to the newly renovated condos next door that the developers bought the mill and shut it down. The mill building is now office space for the Wheat Marketing Center, offering courses like "Wheat Quality Workshop for Nebraska Farmers" and "Asia Noodle Training for Peru" specifically aimed at the worldwide wheat industry.

4.88 mi. Cross NW Naito to NW 9th. In stark contrast to the gleaming condos with reflecting pools next door is the Portland Police Horse Stables, home of the Mounted Patrol Unit (MPU). The nine horses and their officers have been a fixture on the streets of Portland since 1979 and are specially trained to handle large crowds (their size and ability to "herd" people is a major advantage).

4.95 mi. Right on NW Overton. Here you enter the former Northwest Industrial District, now better known as the Pearl, and pass by the Fields Neighborhood Park ❹.

5.03 mi. Turn left on NW 11th (be careful on the streetcar tracks at Northrup) and left again on NW Marshall. Before the second turn is Tanner Springs Park, a re-created wetland mimicking the lake which once covered this area and the natural ecosystem surrounding it.

5.3 mi. Right on NW Station. Pass under the Broadway Bridge and come upon Union Station, built in 1896 in Italian Renaissance style with its 150-foot-tall clock tower (the neon "Go by Train" was added in 1948). When the interior was redesigned in 1927, the mezzanine level was torn out and Italian marble floors and walls were added. The result? A bright, stunning main waiting hall. Go in and see it if you never have before.

5.55 mi. Right on NW Irving and right on NW Broadway. Bike uphill onto the sidewalk and ride across the bridge. You will likely have some company: it has the second highest bridge bike traffic in the city. When completed in 1913 it was the first bascule bridge in Portland and the longest of that type in the world. In 2012 the Portland Streetcar began to run on the Broadway Bridge again after a 55-year absence.

❹

The Fields Neighborhood Park at NW 10th and NW Overton opened in 2013 with the latest in park technology (in other words, lots of areas for different types of recreation, and a really cool playground made of cables and giant woven rope).

Behind the park is the hulking Centennial Mills complex of decayed buildings. Beginning in 1910 with one small waterside mill, the complex grew over the decades to 11 buildings spread over almost five acres. The city bought it in 2000 and has been trying to figure out what to do with it ever since. After spending $13 million developing plans to turn it into an entertainment and shopping extravaganza, the city and developers gave up and here it sits, awaiting a great idea and tens of millions of dollars in investment.

Looming above the park, the spectacular 1973 Fremont Bridge is Portland's response to the aesthetic outrage at the Marquam Bridge, built on a tight budget in 1966. For the Fremont, public opinion was heavily sought and the result was almost six times more expensive. The 15-by-25-foot flags at the top—added for the nation's bicentennial in 1976—can only be reached via an arduous and steep passageway inside the arch. Peregrine falcons, the world's fastest animal and a former endangered species, have nested under the lower deck of the bridge since 1994.

⑤

The Rose Quarter was once the center of Portland's African American community and jazz club district, which started hopping after thousands of African Americans came to Portland to work in the World War II–era shipyards. Clubs like Paul's Paradise, the Frat Hall, the Savoy, Lil' Sandy's, Jackie's, and the Dude Ranch filled the area with the sound of jazz and attracted legendary artists Coleman Hawkins and Thelonius Monk. The area was famed for its round-the-clock activity until much of it was razed to build Memorial Coliseum in 1960 and Interstate 5 in 1966. Today this prime acreage sits empty except for a few hours a day during basketball or hockey season or for concerts, when thousands all want to park at once. I'd rather have the jazz joints.

6.1 mi. As you leave the Broadway Bridge, you enter the 30-acre Rose Quarter **⑤**, whose history has been swept away to make room for sports arenas. Turn right on N Larrabee (the first street after the bridge).

6.23 mi. Left on N Interstate.

6.5 mi. Continue straight across the MAX tracks.

6.6 mi. Cross NE Oregon, ride downhill on the right-hand sidewalk and turn at the first right toward the river. Stop at the top of the ramp for a fantastic view of downtown.

6.72 mi. Descend the ramp (it doubles back on itself) and at the bottom, turn right onto the esplanade. Then turn left onto the Steel Bridge and ride across.

7.05 mi. At the end of the bridge, turn left and ride along the waterfront path.

7.39 mi. Turn right after the Burnside Bridge and glass awning that shelters the Portland Saturday Market. Cross SW Naito at SW Ankeny. Turn right on 1st and walk your bike on the sidewalk.

7.53 mi. Back to the start.

RIDE

OREGON ZOO TO SATURDAY MARKET

STARTING POINT
Washington Park MAX Station (SW Knights Boulevard at the Oregon Zoo)

8.49 miles

DISTANCE

EASY 157 feet

DIFFICULTY & ELEVATION GAIN

SCAVENGER HUNT

Bushes trimmed into the shape of animals

....

A statue of Sacajawea with her arm outstretched and her son, Jean-Baptiste, on her back

....

A "pedal garden" of bike racks with leaf roofs

....

TRANSIT AND PARKING

Washington Park MAX Station (SW Knights Boulevard at the Oregon Zoo)

Transit and parking: TriMet's MAX Red and Blue lines stop at the Washington Park station. TriMet bus 63 and 83 both stop at the MAX elevator. You can park in the pay lot next to the elevators.

The ride ends at the Skidmore Fountain MAX station (1st Avenue under the Burnside Bridge). If you leave a car in the Washington Park lot, take the Red or Blue line train back to the Washington Park MAX station and take the elevator to the top.

WHAT MAKES THIS one-way ride so thrilling and unique? It offers the chance to roll nearly effortlessly from Washington Park's greenery high up in the hills, down past a famous view, through magnificent gardens, and into the city center. To top it off, you'll then ride across two of the city's most beautiful and popular biking bridges and view the whole of what you just rode from the other side of the river.

SPIDER WEB WINDOW
ON SW FAIRVIEW

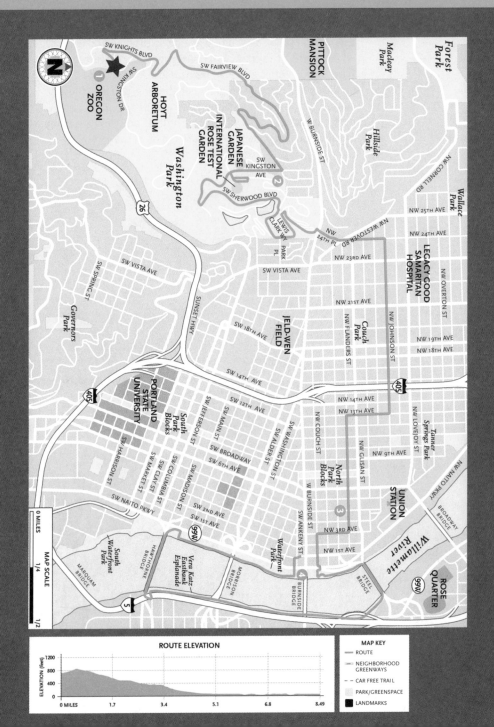

MAP SCALE

0 MILES   1/4   1/2

ROUTE ELEVATION

ELEVATION (feet)

1200
800
400
0

0 MILES   1.7   3.4   5.1   6.8   8.49

MAP KEY

— ROUTE

≈≈≈ NEIGHBORHOOD GREENWAYS

– – CAR FREE TRAIL

PARK/GREENSPACE

■ LANDMARKS

❶

The Oregon Zoo in Washington Park certainly has a wild history. In the late 1880s English native Richard Knight's pharmacy near the Willamette River gained the reputation as a good place for sailors to leave off the animals they'd acquired in their world travels. Knight's collection of cute little critters came to include a grizzly bear staked in the lot next door. Mr. Knight eventually donated the "she-grizzly" to the city and she ended up in a cage in City Park, as Washington Park was then called. That 1888 gift created the oldest zoo west of the Mississippi. Today, more than 1.5 million people a year visit the zoo's thousands of animals in their naturalistic exhibits. Since 1979, summertime concerts have added amplified human mating calls (aka "music") to those of the animals, and during the holidays the zoo dresses up in lights, many visible only from the Zoo Railway.

Zoobombers are another form of wild. They meet every Sunday evening at the Zoobomb Pile sculpture (where bikes are stored) at Burnside and SW 13th and ride the MAX to Washington Park before "bombing" down the hill—repeatedly and often on minibikes—back to the start. Getting to the bottom first is a source of pride, but they go out of their way to be inclusive and encourage safety and fun (and Pabst Blue Ribbon beer, not sure how well all three go together). Keeping Portland weird since 2002, and enduring neighborhood complaints, broken teeth, citations for skipping MAX fare, and unwanted attention from Johnny Law, Zoobombers say they just want to have a good time while showing how much fun riding a bicycle is. Ditto says I. Come to think of it, technically *you* are a Zoobomber—welcome to the club!

0.0 mi. Begin in Washington Park ❶, near the MAX station elevators, and ride uphill on (unmarked) SW Knights. Washington Park is Portland's version of New York's Central Park, only on a steep hillside. And in fact, it was designed with significant input from the Olmsted Brothers, the landscape design company responsible for Central Park. Almost all the climbing on this ride is in the first half mile, but the ride down is worth it. Walking is an option of course. Or, to skip the climb altogether, turn right on SW Kingston and rejoin the route at the International Rose Test Garden.

0.44 mi. Right on SW Fairview. Pass Hoyt Arboretum, an incredible 187-acre urban forest featuring more than 1100 species of plants, and miles of trails for exploration. As you bomb downhill (that is, bomb downhill in a safe and respectful manner) you enter Arlington Heights, which its neighborhood website calls a "museum of architectural styles." The street is steep and narrow, so ride slow, all the better to take in the sights.

1.82 mi. Right on SW Kingston. The tennis courts on the left with rose vines climbing the chain link may have the best view in the city. On your right, the Portland Japanese Garden is a tranquil place to visit during any season.

2.06 mi. Left on SW Kingston Drive. After checking out the roses in the International Rose Test Garden ❷ ride around the parking lot loop and return to the intersection with SW Kingston.

2.24 mi. Left on SW Sherwood. Look up and to the right and you'll see the Washington Park and Zoo Railway which runs for two miles from the Rose Garden to the Oregon Zoo. Soon, pass by the huge play structure of the Rose Garden Children's Park, a great hangout spot for kids and parents, and next door, a picnic shelter, which was an elephant barn in its former life.

2.98 mi. Right at the stop sign at the bottom of the hill (a city water reservoir is on your right). Ride around the loop with its manicured lawns and statues. Continue around the loop at the main entrance (SW Park Pl) where the road name turns into SW Lewis Clark.

3.35 mi. Turn sharply right on the unmarked path with a metal pole in the middle, just across from the elegant two-tiered Chiming Fountain. Be careful on this steep downhill and walk if necessary. In a few yards, take another sharp right on the forested downhill path.

3.64 mi. The path ends at W Burnside. Cross Burnside and continue onto NW 24th Pl.

3.79 mi. Left on NW Westover (at the miniature stop sign) and right on NW 24th Ave, which still has its original brick street.

4 mi. Right on NW Johnson, into the bustling heart of the Alphabet District, so-named for the streets ascending from Ankeny through York. On NW 23rd, stalwarts from the dark days when this was a run-down and seedy neighborhood (like Escape From New York Pizza) have been joined by new boutiques and restaurants. A similar, perhaps slightly more bohemian scene, lies two blocks ahead on NW 21st.

❷

Portland was already nicknamed the Rose City for its natural abundance of roses when, in 1917, a group of nurserymen decided to create a garden here to scientifically test new varieties for color, fragrance, and disease resistance. It also received European varieties in order to save them from possible extinction during World War I. Today, the International Rose Test Garden is a beloved Portland institution. It contains more than 7000 plants of 550 varietals and the city's most famous overlook at the bottom of the garden.

③ ———————————————

The Chinatown gate, erected to welcome Chinese immigrants to Portland, says "Portland Chinatown" in Chinese characters on one side and "Four seas, one family" on the other. Once a bustling immigrant neighborhood with thousands of people packing the streets speaking dozens of languages, Portland's Chinatown slipped into decline in the 1940s as people began moving to the suburbs, leaving today's Chinatown a mostly empty shell. One newer gem, however, is the white-walled Lan Su Chinese Garden (239 NW Everett), modeled after the gardens of Suzhou— Portland's sister city in China's Jiangsu province. Lan Su (*Lan* from Portland and *Su* from Suzhou) was built by sixty-five Chinese artisans using materials from China, including 500 tons of rock, and took more than a year to construct. On the corner of NW 3rd and NW Flanders, in a little plot outside the garden, notice a couple of jagged rocks set in the corner of the wall. These are limestone scholar's stones, eroded into these shapes where they were found in Lake Tai in eastern China. Scholar's stones are highly prized as a subject for traditional Chinese art and as adornments for Chinese gardens.

4.77 mi. Pass under Interstate 405, entering the Pearl District, and turn right on NW 13th. This picturesque street was once a rail line from Union Station, hence the loading docks interspersed with restaurants and shops.

4.96 mi. Left on NW Flanders.

5.3 mi. Cross busy NW Broadway. For an easier crossing, go one block in either direction to a stoplight. Now you're in Old Town Chinatown, Portland's original immigrant district (look right to see the Chinatown Gate as you cross 4th) **③**. A plaque on the red brick building on the corner of Flanders and 4th marks what was once the workshop of the Povey Brothers, crafters of highly prized stained glass windows which still grace many of Portland's beautiful churches and homes.

5.51 mi. Right on NW 3rd.

5.61 mi. Left on NW Couch.

5.86 mi. Cross Naito and turn left at the river onto the waterfront path.

6.1 mi. Turn right to cross the Steel Bridge. This is the second bridge in the same location, both with the same name. The choice to use steel as the building material for the original bridge in 1888 was due to the then-recent catastrophic collapses suffered by other bridges throughout the country made from strong yet brittle cast iron metal.

After crossing, turn right onto the Eastbank Esplanade. Follow the path as it goes down the ramp onto the floating walkway and back up again. At the top of the ramp is a great view of where the ride started at the Oregon Zoo—look to the left of the US Bancorp Tower ("big pink") and near the base of the needle-like radio antennas. Continue on the esplanade, passing under the Morrison Bridge.

7.34 mi. Just before the Hawthorne Bridge, turn left and ride up the ramp. At the top of the ramp, turn right onto the bridge and cross the river again. On the west end of the bridge you'll see the digital bike counter donated in 2012 by Cycle Oregon. How many bikes crossed today?

7.7 mi. Turn right at the end of the bridge and ride around the green building to the Salmon Street Springs Fountain. With more than a hundred jets, this fountain is a popular place to cool down in the summertime. Continue along the river path.

8.44 mi. At the glass-roofed Saturday Market ❹ pavilion (just before the Burnside Bridge) turn left and cross SW Naito on Ankeny.

8.49 mi. Turn right on 1st and walk your bike from here to the Skidmore Fountain MAX station, the end of the ride.

❹

Since 1974, the Portland Saturday Market has run every Saturday—and Sunday—March through Christmas Eve. Each item at the 275 booths is required to be handmade by the seller, and the personalities are as eclectic as the products. Each weekend, people flock from the four corners of the region to browse the goods and enjoy the music, food, river views, and lively atmosphere (also to flirt and show off their latest fighting dogs and tribal tattoos). The market on the other side of Skidmore Fountain is the Skidmore Market, where products don't have to be handcrafted so vendors are free to hawk whatever they imported from developing countries on the cheap. Now that so many fantastic food carts have moved in nearby, the food here seems little better than carnival fare, but the people-watching is unparalleled and entertainers often perform near the fountain as MAX trains periodically roll by.

4 OREGON ZOO TO BEAVERTON

11.05
miles

EASY
174 feet

SCAVENGER
HUNT

STARTING POINT
Washington Park
MAX Station (SW
Knights Boulevard
at the Oregon Zoo)

DISTANCE

**DIFFICULTY &
ELEVATION GAIN**

A 42-ton steam
locomotive
named Peggy

A couple of kissing
donkeys

A front yard log fort

TRANSIT AND PARKING

MAX Red and Blue lines stop at the Washington Park station, the
starting point. TriMet bus 63 and 83 both stop at the MAX elevator.
There's also a pay parking lot next to the elevators.

   The ride ends at TriMet's MAX Beaverton Transit Center (SW
Lombard north of Canyon Road). At the end of the ride, take the
Red or Blue MAX line back to Washington Park. Or find your way to
wherever you want to go on a TriMet bus: lines 20, 52, 53, 54, 57,
58, 61, 76, 78, 88 all stop here.

   Road notes: SW Canyon Road (3.5 miles into the ride) is steep
and lacks a shoulder.

THIS **MOSTLY DOWNHILL,** one-way ride begins 260 feet below ground at the deepest train station in the United States. (A core sample mounted horizontally on the platform wall shows the geologic history from the tunnel to the surface). From lofty Washington Park, the ride winds through layers of neighborhoods: you'll pass forested cottages, modest but neatly kept 1950s ranches, and a street of stately mansions. Down on the Tualatin Valley floor you'll discover numerous wetlands popping up in surprising places. And in a random big-box parking lot you'll find one of the world's most well-regarded training centers for an ancient sport normally associated with the most well-heeled classes. In other words, it's a grand adventure in a part of the metro area that's more bike friendly than you might initially assume.

PEGGY THE TRAIN

The West Slope neighborhood, annexed to Beaverton in 2010, is attached to the city only by Canyon Road. On a city boundary map it resembles a Tootsie pop on a stick. An aerial map of Beaverton looks like a corn maze—curving roads with orderly grids inside the curves of irregularly shaped triangles—making the area interesting, confusing, secretive, tucked-away, cozy, rural, fascinating, and maddening at the same time. City boundaries are more squiggles and hiccups, often running only one building deep on a road ending in a bulb surrounded by unincorporated county.

0.0 mi. The starting point for this ride is the subterrestrial MAX station at Washington Park. Take the elevator up: instead of the floor, the display shows the height above sea level for the tunnel and surface (450 up to 693 feet). Exit the station and head downhill on unmarked SW Knights.

0.45 mi. At the bottom of the hill, just before Highway 26, turn right onto SW Canyon Court at the sign marked "Sylvan." After the turn, you'll pass an entrance to the 30-mile Wildwood Trail (for walkers only) from Washington Park to the north end of Forest Park. The piney scent from the forest softens the jarring roar of the freeway to your left.

1.11 mi. Just before the stop sign where Canyon turns into SW Westgate, turn left onto the multi-use path that runs alongside Highway 26.

This neighborhood, Sylvan-Highlands, has been called "the leafiest neighborhood in Portland." Sylvan comes from the word *Sylvanus*, or "Roman deity of the woods." These hills may be short on Roman deities but the woods are plentiful. Transmission towers to your right sit 1100 feet above sea level and rise another 1000 feet into the sky.

1.3 mi. Cross SW Skyline and continue on the path.

2.02 mi. Follow the path to the left as it crosses over Highway 26, and as it turns right on SW Pointer.

2.34 mi. Right onto the path at SW 75th.

2.88 mi. Left at the sign above Highway 26 marked "Exit 69B–St. Vincent Hospital" and left again on SW Katherine. Continue on the road as it turns right and becomes SW 84th. This is the West Slope neighborhood ❶.

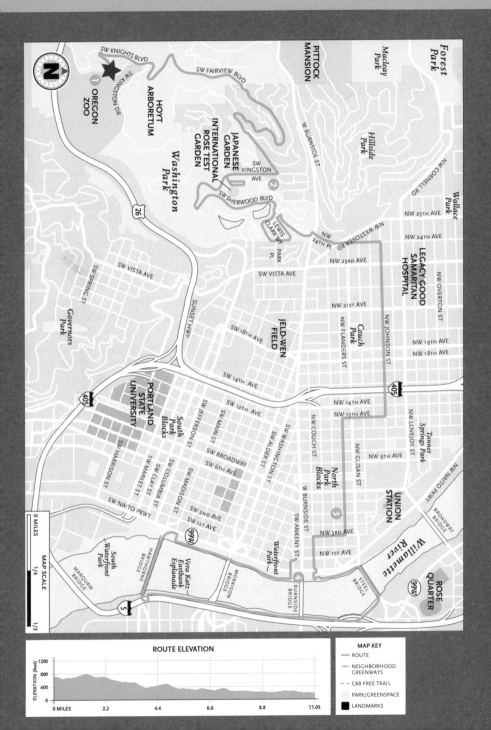

MAP SCALE

0 MILES   1/4   1/2

ROUTE ELEVATION

MAP KEY
ROUTE
NEIGHBORHOOD GREENWAYS
CAR FREE TRAIL
PARK/GREENSPACE
LANDMARKS

2

Have you noticed the "Canyon" theme to the street names around here? I like to think of riding a bicycle as the closest thing to driving a wagon of grain up and over the mountains (at least it feels that way with my daughter in the trailer behind, and you know who the "ox team" is). Canyon Road was once known as the Great Plank Road and is mostly responsible for Portland becoming the center of the region's economy. In the early days of the Oregon Territory, the Tualatin Mountains were the biggest obstacle between the fertile, grain-rich Tualatin Valley and the ocean-going ships waiting in the Willamette River. The entrepreneurs of Portland, then just a clearing in the woods on the banks of the Willamette, put wooden planks on enough portions of a muddy road deep in the canyons of the mountains that valley farmers preferred it to the 3 to 10 extra miles on roads to rivaling towns St. Johns or St. Helens.

3.3 mi. Left on SW Schiller and right on SW Valley View.

3.5 mi. Right on SW Canyon Lane. Warning: it's steep and has no shoulder, but at least you're going downhill.

3.83 mi. Left on SW 87th (at the sign marked "To SW 87th Ave, Post Office"). Here, the community center of West Slope has a small cluster of shops with a few options for food and pit stops.

4 mi. Cross SW 87th and turn left on SW Canyon Road.

4.08 mi. Right on SW Canyon Dr (unmarked soft right after one block). This quiet, green country road is welcome after the unpleasant crossing of Canyon Rd **2**.

4.82 mi. Right on SW Ridgewood.

5.09 mi. Right on the path signed "Raleigh Park & Swim Center." This nice neighborhood park greets you immediately with a small stream complete with footbridges and an outdoor pool.

5.36 mi. Left on SW 78th. Get some steam going for the short, steep hill or just walk it.

5.78 mi. Cross SW Beaverton-Hillsdale Highway into the parking lot behind Raleigh Hills Plaza. This mini-mall has a charming mix of chain and local stores that would fit in on a main street in the smallest town. Ride straight through to SW Scholls Ferry.

6.26 mi. Right on Scholls Ferry.

6.82 mi. Right on the unmarked street (SW Old Scholls Ferry) across from the stately brick building on the left, the Portland Golf Club.

7.4 mi. Right on Scholls Ferry and right again on SW Elm. You'll find a bunch of small shops and restaurants at this little intersection.

8.43 mi. Left on SW Chestnut and left again on the unmarked path (which becomes SW 5th) immediately before tucked-away McMillan Park.

8.6 mi. Turn right into the parking lot just before SW Western (the sidewalk is very narrow and the street is not fit for bicycles). Ride through the parking lot and get back on the sidewalk just before the KFC. It's hard to miss the giant fencers, epee in hand, on the side of the Northwest Fencing Center. This is where Beaverton's own two-time Olympic gold medalist, Mariel Zagunis, trains. The center, home to the U.S. National Fencing team, attracts new and seasoned fencers from around the world. Nearby, another large sign invites you to play a more familiar and hopefully less deadly sport, billiards.

8.86 mi. Turn left on SW Beaverton-Hillsdale Highway (activate the light by pressing the crosswalk button) and turn right on SW 103rd.

9.08 mi. Left on SW Kennedy. On your right, the unassuming ditch is one of Beaverton's three principal creeks, Hall Creek. The presence of Hall Creek is a good reminder that the valley's waterways, a main reason the pioneers travelled 2000 miles to get here, are still a valuable part of our natural environment and their health and cleanliness is up to us all.

③

Beaverton's three creeks join up near Center Street Park, creating this wetland, the others you've seen, and more you'd have trouble finding because they're in an underground maze of pipes, around parking lots, and running down ditches on little back streets. The City of Beaverton has realized this forgotten natural resource can be a way to revitalize the downtown area, making it more pedestrian and bicycle friendly and breaking "down the wall of automobile traffic." They've created the Three Creeks Confluence plan, with Beaverton Creek acting as a central spine connecting a series of green spaces, walking paths, and bike trails with walkways, bridges, benches and retail shops. The crowning achievement would be to create a series of canals, like Venice, Italy (or Venice, California!). Stay tuned.

9.25 mi. Right on SW 107th.

9.4 mi. Left on SW Canyon and right on SW 108th.

9.86 mi. Left on SW Polsky and left on SW 110th.

10.08 mi. Turn right on SW Cabot which curves left to become 113th and then right to become SW Center. About a half mile later (at SW 117th) Center Street Park ❸ is on your right.

10.83 mi. Left on SW Lombard.

11.02 mi. Left into the MAX Beaverton Transit Center (if you get to SW Canyon, you've gone too far). As you roll into the MAX station, look to your left to see the transmission antennas way back up on Sylvan-Highlands where the ride began.

11.05 mi. This is the end of the ride. If you left a car in the Washington Park lot, take the Red or Blue line train back to the Washington Park MAX station and take the elevator to the top.

5 WASHINGTON COUNTY: OLD RAILWAY, NEW GREENWAY

THE HIGHLIGHT OF this ride is the car-free Fanno Creek Greenway Trail, which glides and weaves alongside the creek bed—between houses and warehouses; through parks, parking lots, and groves of waterlogged trees; and past ponds full of ducks and open meadows—begging to be explored. This decades-long work-in-progress is a treasure for local communities, and when completed, will be another jewel in the crown of Portland-area multi-use paths.

Ask Southwest suburban Portland residents why they live on the west side and many cite the schools, the hilly terrain, the country feel, safety, the great neighborhood parks— oh, and lower taxes relative to Portland. This ride takes you through a patchwork of west side Washington County cities and communities—including Beaverton, Tigard, and unincorporated Metzger and Garden Home—to discover what people who live here like so much about their neighborhoods.

SCAVENGER HUNT

A roadside library on a post: "Take Books or Leave Books"

·····················

A big tree stump with roots lying on its side

·····················

A chimney with a scarab (beetle) on it

·····················

STARTING POINT

Tigard Transit
Center WES Station
(8960 SW Commer-
cial Street, Tigard
97223)

11.11
miles

DISTANCE

MODERATE
243 feet

DIFFICULTY &
ELEVATION GAIN

TRANSIT AND
PARKING

TriMet's WES train
serves the Tigard
Transit Center from
the Beaverton Transit
Center. TriMet buses
12, 76, 78, and 94 stop
right at the Transit
Center. Street parking
is available along SW
Commercial and SW
Main.

CAMILLE PARK

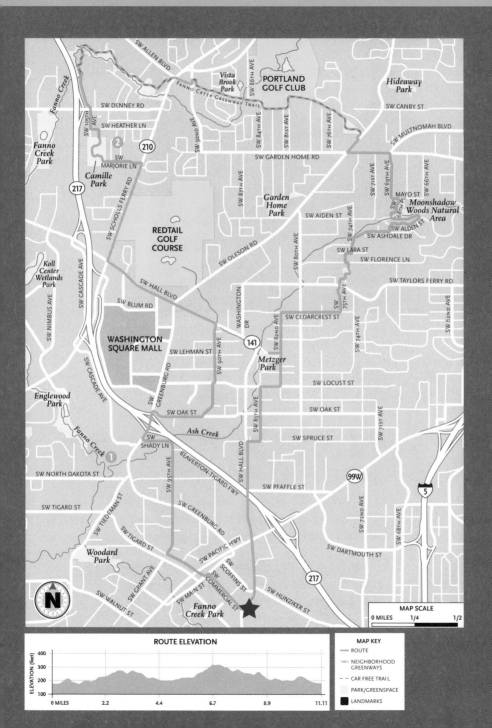

ROUTE ELEVATION

MAP KEY
— ROUTE
≈ NEIGHBORHOOD GREENWAYS
-- CAR FREE TRAIL
▭ PARK/GREENSPACE
■ LANDMARKS

MAP SCALE
0 MILES   1/4   1/2

Fanno Creek is 15 miles long with 14 tributaries and more than a dozen parks along its length. With headwaters near Council Crest in the Tualatin Mountains, it's considered a sub-basin of the Tualatin River watershed. Fanno Creek is useful, not only for its parks and green space in the city, but also as a measure of overall groundwater pollution. In 1995 the Oregon Department of Environmental Quality raised the creek's water rating from "very poor" to "poor": a promising trajectory.

0.0 mi. Ride north on SW Commercial (left with the transit center at your back) away from the Tigard Transit Center. Tigard was originally settled by Wilson Tigard of Arkansas in 1852 as Tigardville but the name was shortened in 1908 by the Oregon Electric Railway to avoid confusion with nearby Wilsonville.

0.08 mi. At Main, turn left and then right to stay on Commercial.

0.31 mi. Right on SW 95th. Cross busy SW Greenburg carefully.

0.95 mi. As you approach Highway 217, 95th turns left and becomes SW Shady Lane. Look to the left for your first glimpse of Fanno Creek ❶.

1.13 mi. Right on Greenburg. Stay in the bike lane that runs between the right turn lane and through lanes.

1.3 mi. After crossing the highway turn right on SW Oak.

1.6 mi. Left on SW 90th.

1.83 mi. At SW Locust, turn right and then left to stay on 90th. Here you enter the unincorporated community of Metzger. Partly annexed into Tigard, the rest of Metzger (.7 square miles and just over 3000 people) is happy to remain free of the taxation and bureaucracy of city-dom, preferring the simplicity and community spirit of answering to only the county.

2.17 mi. Left on SW Hall. The big box stores you see after crossing Greenburg are part of Washington Square Mall's nearly 1.5 million square feet. The RedTail public golf course on your right (named for the hawks nesting in nearby trees) provides entertainment on the opposite end of the spectrum.

2.91 mi. Right on SW Scholls Ferry.

3.53 mi. Left on SW Marjorie just before McKay School.

3.78 mi. When Marjorie dead ends at Camille Park , turn right onto the park's path. Turn left at the playground and ride clockwise around the boardwalk. Then turn left on the main path and exit the park on SW 104th.

4.06 mi. Left on SW Heather and right on SW 105th. Be careful crossing busy SW Denney.

4.45 mi. Where SW 105th dead-ends, join the Fanno Creek Greenway Trail. This first section alone contains 11 boardwalks over wetlands or creeks on the 10-foot-wide gloriously wild trail.

4.62 mi. Turn right after the long bridge.

5.28 mi. When this section of trail ends, stay right and ride around the parking lot, arriving at the intersection of SW Scholls Ferry and SW Allen. Turn right on Allen. If you're not comfortable riding on Allen, use the sidewalk on the left side.

5.48 mi. Left on SW 92nd to rejoin the Fanno Creek Greenway. This romantic and secret section of trail, with its tunnel of shrubs and trees, feels like you should be riding on a high-spirited stallion in your red fox hunting outfit accompanied by a pack of hounds. Or maybe that's just me. Less than a half mile later, pass the Portland Golf Club behind the tall black fence.

6.59 mi. Right on SW Oleson (at the athletic fields and parking lot). Here's the community of Garden Home–Whitford, two more stops on the Oregon Electric Railway. What is now the Garden Home Recreation Center was built in 1912 as a school.

More than just a playground and tennis courts, 12-acre Camille Park has a camas lily meadow and one of the last habitats of Oregon white oak, which has declined to less than 15 percent of its original range in the state. Here, park staff cleared out other tree species to give them more light and removed nonnative English ivy and Himalayan blackberry. The camas lily is also native to the Northwest; the bulb was once the main food source for Native Americans and settlers in the region. The 1- to 2-foot-tall plant covers open meadows in spring with light blue flowers. A 700-foot-long boardwalk winds through the wetland where you might hear a chorus of native frogs looking for love in the restored habitat. Got kids? The park's playground contains a fun fake hollow log, a real giant tree stump on its side, and a series of jumbled logs bolted together, all enticing to young climbers.

6.74 mi. Left on SW Garden Home (use the crosswalk). A sign declares "Welcome to Portland."

6.99 mi. Right on SW 69th. As it turns left it becomes SW Mayo.

7.29 mi. Right on SW 68th Pl. Continue to the short gravel path at the left side of the cul-de-sac and enter Moonshadow Woods Natural Area (there's no curb cut to the path). The park straddles Ash Creek and a 1996 restoration included installing boulders and the "woody debris" that fish need for shelter and spawning.

7.43 mi. Left after the bridge over Ash Creek and follow the trail through the park. As the trail turns right, be ready for the steep hill exiting the park.

7.6 mi. Right on SW Alden.

7.83 mi. Right on SW Ashdale.

8.05 mi. Left on SW 74th.

8.14 mi. Right on SW Lara and left on SW 75th.

8.24 mi. Left on SW Florence and then turn right on the path into tiny Florence Pointe Park.

8.31 mi. At the little path before the bridge, turn right to exit the park. Then turn right on unmarked SW Herb. After crossing SW Taylors Ferry, Herb becomes SW 75th.

8.57 mi. Right on SW Cedarcrest.

8.94 mi. Left on SW 82nd and right into Metzger Park. The park's Patricia D. Whiting Hall is named for a longtime community activist and state legislator whose accomplishments include preserving the park as well as Metzger's independence (from Tigard). Ride through the parking lot (and explore as you wish) before returning to 82nd.

9.36mi. From 82nd, turn right on SW Locust.

9.48 mi. Left on SW 85th. The large house on the corner of Spruce and 85th is the Cordero House, a residential program for a dozen boys aged 14 to 19 who've
been victims of abuse. From 2009 to 2011, local builders
donated almost two years' time and more than half of
the $800,000 needed to upgrade the 90-year-old house
with new walls and floors, updated showers, and a new
hot water heater. Now that's community spirit.

9.79 mi. Right on SW Spruce and left on SW Hall (the
sidewalk is a good alternative on busy Hall). After crossing SW Highway 99/Pacific Highway, be careful of the
deep storm grates on the right.

10.84 mi. Right on SW Commercial.

11.11 mi. Back to the start.

 BEAVERTON'S PONDS, PARKS, AND POWER-LINE TRAIL

10.49 miles

EASY 148 feet

STARTING POINT
Elmonica/SW 170th Ave MAX Station (SW 170th Avenue and Baseline Road, Beaverton 97006)

DISTANCE

DIFFICULTY & ELEVATION GAIN

Six duck ponds

....

A house that looks like a castle with a lava stone "tower" entrance

....

A bike rack shaped like a fire truck

....

TRANSIT AND PARKING

Transit and parking: TriMet's MAX Blue Line stops at the Elmonica/SW 170th Ave station. No bus service. Street parking is very scarce here, try Baseline between 162nd and 163rd.

ROAD NOTES There's no bike lane on Baseline which the route traverses briefly at the beginning and end of the ride.

BEAVERTON COULD BE called the city of parks. You'll
spend the first half of this ride on car-free paths
inside several wildly different parks, including an open
area under powerlines, the "crown jewel" sports complex of the Tualatin Hills Park & Recreation District, a
boardwalk through a wetland greenway, and even a couple of residential lakes. After that, you'll ride through
farmland-turned-residential areas that have developed
since the 1950s, and also catch a glimpse of the headquarters of Oregon's sporty Fortune 500 company.

WATERHOUSE LAKE

As the name suggests, Waterhouse Powerline Park runs along the path of powerlines. Currently 8 miles long, it's part of the 25-mile Westside Trail planned to eventually extend from the St. Johns Bridge, over the Tualatin Mountains, and south through the valley to the Tualatin River, to become one of the longest car-free pathways in the area (that is if all landowners, including Nike, allow easements across their land). Since buildings can't be placed under powerlines, and they tower over long stretches of open space, they are ideal for pathways. The only glitch is the negative press powerlines have received around the potential health dangers their electromagnetic fields might pose to people. So far, studies have failed to show any connection, so fear not bold rider, your brain is safe—assuming you're wearing a helmet. More immediate dangers include downed powerlines from falling trees or drunk drivers hitting poles. If for some bizarre reason you find yourself near a downed powerline, you should shuffle away, as a raised foot can create a circuit.

0.0 mi. Begin at the Elmonica/SW 170th Ave MAX station and ride away from the station platform, through the parking lot to SW Jenkins. This MAX stop retains the Oregon Electric Railroad's original station name. The farmer who owned the land around here would only allow the railroad to build through his property if the stop was named after his daughters, Eleanor and Monica. Hence: Elmonica.

0.17 mi. Cross SW Jenkins and continue on W Baseline. There's no bike lane on Baseline so consider riding on the sidewalk.

0.32 mi. At the sign for "Waterhouse South Powerline Park," turn left on the path that runs underneath the powerlines. ❶

0.85 mi. Cross SW Walker and continue on the bike path.

1.02 mi. Turn left after the bridge (look for the RV and boat storage parking lot on the left). This brings you into Five Oaks, a neighborhood with ritzy and medieval-looking Tudor-style mansions among more traditional Northwest-style homes.

1.23 mi. Left on NW 167th and right on NW Walker. The intermittent sidewalk might be a better choice than the bike lane on this busy road.

1.42 mi. Right on NW 170th. Ride one block and then turn left to stay on NW 170th.

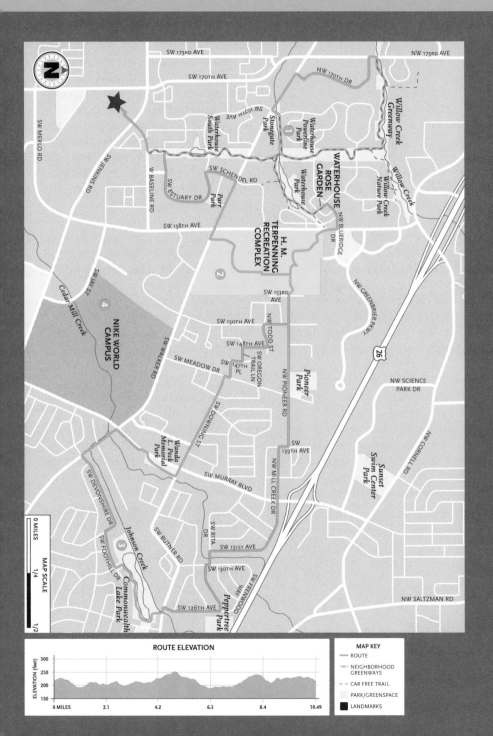

SW 173RD AVE
NW 173RD AVE
SW 170TH AVE
NW 170TH DR
NW 170TH DR
SW MERLO RD
SW 167TH AVE
Waterhouse South Park
Stonegate Park
Waterhouse Powerline Park
WATERHOUSE ROSE GARDEN
Willow Creek Greenway
Willow Creek Nature Park
Willow Creek
SW SWENNING RD
W BASELINE RD
W BASELINE RD
SW ESTUARY DR
SW SCHENDEL RD
Waterhouse Park
NW BLUERIDGE DR
SW 158TH AVE
Parr Park
H. M. TERPENNING RECREATION COMPLEX
NW GREENBRIER PKWY
Cedar Mill Creek
SW JAY ST
NIKE WORLD CAMPUS
SW 153RD AVE
SW 150TH AVE
NW TODD ST
NW SCIENCE PARK DR
26
SW 148TH AVE
SW WALKER RD
SW MEADOW DR
SW 147TH PL
SW OREGON TRAIL LN
NW PIONEER RD
Pioneer Park
NW CORNELL RD
SW DOWNING ST
Wanda L. Peck Memorial Park
SW SWINNING ST
SW 139TH AVE
NW MILL CREEK DR
Sunset Swim Center Park
SW DEVONSHIRE DR
SW MURRAY BLVD
SW RITA DR
SW 131ST AVE
Johnson Creek
SW BUTNER RD
SW 130TH AVE
SW FREMONT WAY
SW FOOTHILL DR
Commonwealth Lake Park
SW 126TH AVE
Peppertree Park
NW SALTZMAN RD

0 MILES
MAP SCALE
1/4
1/2

ROUTE ELEVATION

ELEVATION (feet)
300
250
200
150

0 MILES   2.1   4.2   6.3   8.4   10.49

MAP KEY
— ROUTE
〜 NEIGHBORHOOD GREENWAYS
- - - CAR FREE TRAIL
　　PARK/GREENSPACE
■ LANDMARKS

1.88 mi. Right on NW 173rd and right on the path marked "Winthrop Path at Willow Creek." Notice the word "bike" has been painted over to make the sign more inclusive. Short Willow Creek Greenway is on a raised boardwalk along the banks of Willow Creek and its wetland. It may be a well-kept secret among the masses, but judging from the number of walkers, joggers, and baby strollers, the locals know a good thing when they live near one. Because of the high traffic and narrow walkway go slowly, ride courteously, and watch out for wildlife, like the garter snake I almost ran over. The plastic walkway of the boardwalk can also be slippery.

2.4 mi. Right at the Y intersection under the powerlines.

2.9 mi. Turn left after the bridge and RV parking lot. On your left, over the fence, you'll see Waterhouse Lake with its fountains, gazebo, waterfall, and resident ducks. In a few yards you'll come to a bridge over a narrow neck of the lake where you can get a good view.

3.25 mi. Left at the Y intersection and pass by small but rosy Waterhouse Rose Garden.

3.32 mi. Right on NW Blueridge. At the intersection with NW 158th, cross the street and turn sharply right on the sidewalk along 158th.

3.54 mi. Turn left into the park (by the roller hockey rink) and take a right after the skate park, entering the H.M. Terpenning Recreation Complex (HMT) of the Tualatin Hills Park & Recreation District (THPRD) ❷. The acronyms are fittingly impressive for this remarkable space.

3.7 mi. Turn left after the baseball field (before the bridge over Waterhouse Creek). Keep the creek on your right and continue on the path, exiting the park on NW Pioneer. If you're wondering why leaving the HMT feels like a magical transport into the countryside—the roadside abruptly ends in a ditch and grassy fields in front of the houses—the reason is that you just left Beaverton and entered unincorporated Washington County. Look for goats in the field a few doors down.

2

Tualatin Hills Park & Recreation District was founded in 1955 as a result of efforts by physical education instructor Elsie Stuhr. At that time the 3000 residents of Beaverton had only two parks, no tennis courts, and the closest place to swim was Forest Grove or Portland. Stuhr foresaw the rapid development of Tualatin Valley's farmlands and knew residents of Beaverton and their future neighbors would want places to relax, enjoy nature, and play. She might have been surprised that, as of 2013, THPRD serves more than 220,000 residents of Beaverton and unincorporated areas of eastern Washington County from Rock Creek and Hillsboro to Tigard. It administers hundreds of parks, trails, streams, lakes, soccer fields, and tennis courts, and offers 3000 classes a year. The Tualatin Hills Nature Park, for example, is a 222-acre wildlife preserve on land once owned by the catholic church that now showcases the area's variety of forest, wetlands and native plants.

The crown jewel of THPRD is the H. M. Terpenning Recreation Complex (HMT), 92 acres of first-class physically active fun named for Howard Terpenning, general manager of THPRD for 33 years, and the site of the first park offices. THPRD bought an additional 66 acres from the Waterhouse family farm and dedicated the center in 1979. Today, HMT features 15 tennis courts (eight outdoor courts are converted to indoor during the winter months with air tents), three sand-based soccer fields, five softball fields, two baseball fields with scoreboards, two skate parks (ESPN broadcast the B3 event—bikes, boards, and blades—at its opening in 1999), a roller hockey rink, six indoor basketball courts, a 50-meter pool with diving platforms, a 10-acre natural area with walking trails, and two synthetic turf fields for soccer, football, and lacrosse. The pizza parlor next door must make a killing!

4.29 mi. Pass by Pioneer Park on your left. The restoration of its wetlands and grounds was completed by THPRD in 2013, and exploring the wild trails of the natural area is a fun side trip.

4.57 mi. Right on NW 139th and left on NW Mill Creek.

4.83 mi. Cross Murray (use the crosswalk at this notoriously dangerous intersection) and continue on Mill Creek, which becomes SW 131st as it curves right.

③

Manmade Common-
wealth Lake was created
in 1965 as an amenity for
the Cedar Hills neigh-
borhood, the single larg-
est housing tract devel-
opment in the country
when it was built in 1961.
The lake, given to THPRD
in 1969, is set on John-
son Creek and stocked
with rainbow trout in
spring, and bass, blue-
gill, and crappie in the
summer for fishermen to
enjoy. In 2013 it under-
went a restoration to
restore native habitat
and rebuild the banks of
the lake, which had been
seriously eroded by eager
fisher-folk. Restoration
included removing the
delicious but very inva-
sive Himalayan black-
berry and planting more
than 3000 native plants
and trees. The lake is
also popular with migrat-
ing birds, and wild ducks
have interbred with the
domestic ones to cre-
ate interestingly colored
crossbreeds that look
ready to jump into your
arms in order to inves-
tigate your pockets for
crumbs.

5.4 mi. Left on SW Rita. Note the deep, dark, jungle-like greenery of Cedar Mill Creek as you cross it. At SW 130th, turn right and then left to stay on Rita.

5.69 mi. Right on SW Frenwood (this becomes SW 126th).

5.94 mi. Left on SW Buttner and right into Commonwealth Lake Park **③**. Ride along the south side of the lake on the path.

6.36 mi. Exit the park at the opposite end of the lake and turn right on SW Foothill.

6.55 mi. Right on SW Devonshire.

6.95 mi. Right on SW Walker (another spot with a decent bike lane, busy traffic, and intermittent sidewalks). Just before the intersection with Murray, Cedar Mill Creek crosses under the roads and continues where we may not: through the headquarters of perhaps the most famous athletic shoe company in the world— Nike **④**.

7.14 mi. Right on SW Murray.

7.3 mi. Get up on the sidewalk at the apartment complex before turning right into Wanda L. Peck Memorial Park. Ride on the path through this unassuming little park, named after the land owner's mother.

7.46 mi. Left on SW Buttner; continue on as it becomes SW Downing.

7.96 mi. Right on SW Meadow, then immediately left onto the car-free path (gravel for just a few feet) and right on SW 147th.

8.12 mi. Turn left on SW Oregon Trail, right on SW 148th, left on NW Todd, and right on SW 150th.

8.62 mi. Left on SW Pioneer. This brings you back to HMT.

8.85 mi. Left at the first bridge over the creek across from Field #3.

8.95 mi. At the T intersection, turn right. Then quickly turn left and ride uphill through the forest.

9.1 mi. Right after the outdoor tennis courts (or blue tents in winter).

9.23 mi. Left in the parking lot and right on SW Walker.

9.58 mi. Left on SW Schendel.

9.75 mi. Left on SW Estuary. As you ride on Estuary, pass little forested Parr Park on the left, a ribbon of natural greenery caught between the mini-mall and apartment complex.

10.25 mi. Left onto the path in Waterhouse South Powerline Park. Follow the path briefly and then turn right on SW Baseline.

10.49 mi. Ride straight across SW Jenkins and back to the start.

4

Founded in 1964 by Phil Knight and University of Oregon track and field coach Bill Bowerman, Nike's 7000-employee, 193-acre campus is literally surrounded by the city of Beaverton, though the property itself is unincorporated. Nike fought off an attempt by the city in 2005 to annex it, winning a legislative decree banning the city from further attempts to plunder it for taxes for 35 years. The main entry road onto campus is 1 Bowerman Drive, in honor of coach Bowerman, whose experiments to create running shoes using a waffle iron gave Phil Knight the idea to start making shoes. In 2011, Coach Bowerman's original waffle iron was found in the landfill behind his home in eastern Oregon and is now on display here at the headquarters. Another interesting fact: Bowerman is also credited with introducing "jogging" to the United States after seeing the newly invented concept at a colleague's training camp in New Zealand. The buildings on campus are named for famous Nike-sponsored athletes including John McEnroe, Michael Jordan, Nolan Ryan, Mia Hamm, and Steve Prefontaine. The campus and the surrounding track are not officially open to the public. I've heard conflicting stories about people checking it out: some say they got kicked out, some didn't. It's your call.

ORENCO AND HILLSBORO'S SILICON FOREST

9.95 miles

EASY 128 feet

SCAVENGER HUNT

STARTING POINT
Quatama/NW 205th
Ave MAX Station
(350 NW 205th
Avenue, Hillsboro
97006)

DISTANCE

DIFFICULTY & ELEVATION GAIN

A fountain with water jets

An eight-sided barn

A round sandstone rock for climbing

TRANSIT AND PARKING

TriMet's MAX Blue Line stops at the Quatama/NW 205th station. There's no close bus service. Look for street parking on NW Quatama.

A **CONESTOGA WAGON** pulls up to a stream in a green meadow. Soon an orchard appears. Time goes by and the orchard's derelict farmhouse is bulldozed to build a community of homes, a strip mall, or a factory. The transition from meadow to farm to city is as old as cities themselves. On this ride through Hillsboro, we'll see evidence of this evolution from virgin countryside to city, including an 1850s-era farmstead turned entertainment hotspot. Hillsboro is home to Oregon's largest employer—and other big names in the Silicon Forest—and has an award-winning mixed-use and transit-oriented community, all of which is interspersed with great parks, creeks, and preserved wetlands.

THE OCTAGONAL BARN AT CORNELIUS PASS ROADHOUSE

Even with a whopping 27 streams running into it, the Tualatin River meanders through the Tualatin Valley before emptying into the Willamette. While 80 percent of the river runs through forest or farmland, the other 20 percent lies in populated areas. Because of its slow movement through prime real estate, these waterways have become a target for draining and pollution, just as other watersheds in earlier developed areas of the region have been. But this area's late blooming has proved to be its savior. Heightened awareness around the importance of water quality and wildlife habitat has brought with it greater efforts to save and restore what we have left.

0.0 mi. Begin at the Quatama/NW 205th Ave MAX station and turn right on NW Quatama Road. Here is the first and maybe best example on the tour of the new and old development checkerboard: roadside ditches and farmer's fields next to townhomes, sidewalks, curbs, and bike lanes.

0.61 mi. Left on NW Cornelius Pass. As you dip down and cross the bridge, a sign points out the Tualatin watershed ❶, visible on both sides. The open space to your left is part of Lexington Park.

1.18 mi. Right on W Baseline. On the corner is a common sight throughout the valley—a sliver of wetland protected behind a chain link fence. As you ride on Baseline, you'll go over Beaverton Creek and then Rock Creek.

2.12 mi. Still on Baseline, pass Noble Woods Park, which contains forest and wetlands straddling Rock Creek. In 1991, when the city bond measure to purchase the land failed, 200 local residents each ponied up $2000 to help create the park. Bikes are unfortunately banned on the mile-long paved trail because, according to a park employee, local school kids were riding too fast on its steep paths.

2.51 mi. Right on NE 55th.

2.79 mi. Left on NE Hidden Creek.

2.9 mi. Left into 53rd Avenue Community Park, which is oriented to the uber-active. The contrast with Noble Woods is striking: raw nature versus the latest in curated activity architecture. Hillsboro residents are lucky and smart enough to have both. Return the way you came and turn left on Hidden Creek.

3.26 mi. Right on NE 53rd.

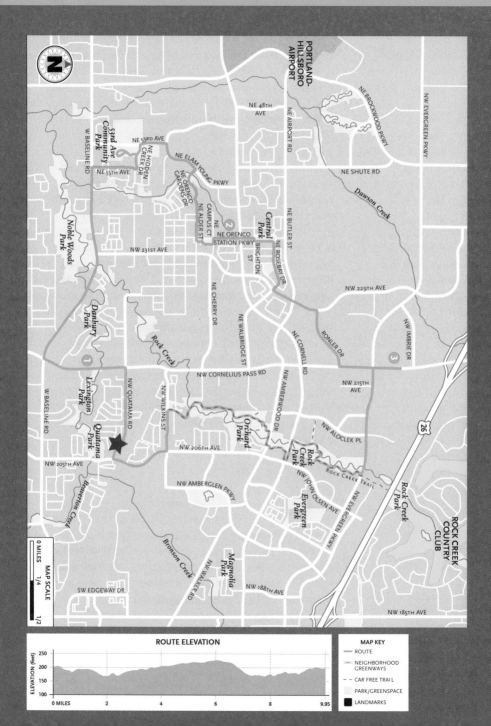

ROUTE ELEVATION

MAP KEY

— ROUTE

≈≈≈ NEIGHBORHOOD GREENWAYS

- - CAR FREE TRAIL

PARK/GREENSPACE

■ LANDMARKS

②————————————————

The Oregon Nursery Company started with 640 acres filled with fruit and nut trees and berries in 1905. Over the years, the company expanded to 1200 acres and built the largest packing shed in the country—two acres under one roof. In 1908, the 500-person town of Orenco was incorporated, but a large capital investment was derailed by World War I and the company went out of business in 1927. All that's left of old Orenco are a few tree-lined blocks of Craftsman homes a few blocks to the east. As the surrounding fields have been gobbled up by housing divisions, and as traffic increases, the sidewalk-less residents have become increasingly trapped in their homes, an island of calm in a raging sea of traffic. The residents, many of whom moved here decades ago for the peace and quiet of a small town, have been resisting the sale of large parcels of land to developers, but change seems inevitable.

Today's Orenco Station was built on the principles of New Urbanism: walkable neighborhoods with houses, shops, and parks. It also takes into consideration the architecture of housing, public spaces, community buildings and landscaping that celebrates local history, climate and ecology. The movement arose in the early 1980s in an attempt to return to city planning principles from the 1920s—that is, before the rise of the automobile.

3.43 mi. Right on NE Elam Young. Now we start to get into the heart of Hillsboro's Silicon Forest. Ever since the first technology company, Tektronix, settled here in 1951, the area has attracted similar companies and now boasts more than 50,000 jobs. You'll probably see a few technology names you recognize.

3.7 mi. Right on NE Orenco Gardens.

3.94 mi. Left on NE Alder. No, it's not London or Paris. This is Orenco Station, named for the Oregon Nursery Company whose town once stood here **②**.

4.22 mi. Left after the leasing office and clubhouse for Orenco Gardens, cross the MAX tracks, and turn right on unmarked Orenco Station.

4.34 mi. Left on NE Campus and right on Orenco Station. As you ride, notice the mixed-use building with apartments above and shops below. The short block after crossing busy NE Cornell is an urban dweller's dream, with small shops behind wide sidewalks and lush landscaping, ripe for browsing shops or lingering over a latte while people watching. The parking lot to the left hosts a farmers market on Sundays, May through October.

4.64 mi. Right on NE Brighton and left on Orenco Station past the wide green expanse of Central Park.

4.79 mi. Right on NE Rosebay. The houses around you show how far planned communities have come. After 40 years of sawdust and plywood building materials, houses can once again look beautiful, only today without laying waste to entire forests. Also, notice the presence of some sort of park or green space on each block.

5.1 mi. Left on NW 229th.

5.27 mi. After you cross NE Butler, on the left, behind the wall-like berm and acres of parking, you'll see the Ronler Acres campus of Intel, Oregon's largest employer (15,000 as of 2013). Founded in 1968 and still headquartered in California, the semiconductor manufacturer built its first plant in Hillsboro in 1979, and Ronler Acres in 1994. To the right you can see Intel's newest facility or "fab" D1X, due to start production in 2015. At 2.5 million square feet, it will cost over $3 billion to build and employ more than 6000 people in its research facility.

5.45 mi. Right on NW Ronler and onto the nice raised bike path.

5.85 mi. Left on busy NW Cornelius Pass.

6.1 mi. At NW Evergreen use the crosswalk and continue up the opposite sidewalk to visit Cornelius Pass Roadhouse & Imbrie Hall ❸. Explore before returning the way you came along Cornelius Pass.

6.3 mi. Left on NW Evergreen. Use the crosswalk again and ride on the sidewalk for the first block to NW 215th.

7.31 mi. Turn right on Rock Creek Trail (after the wetland behind the low rock wall). Immediately, the roar of cars gives way to bird calls. A work in progress, Rock Creek Trail is a wonderful half-finished masterpiece. We hit the trail midway through but it continues on to the north, running past a great blue heron rookery and underneath Highway 26. The grand plan is to extend the trail for a total of 6 miles, all the way to Rock Creek's confluence with the Tualatin River.

③

Of all the McMenamins properties, Cornelius Pass Roadhouse & Imbrie Hall may have grown the most spectacularly from relatively humble beginnings. From 1850 to 1988, this 6-acre property belonged to generations of the Imbrie family who raised Morgan draft horses, dairy cows, sheep, chickens, and hogs (and grew wheat, hay, oats, and barley) on their 1500-acre farm. In 1986, the McMenamins brothers, known for turning historic buildings into temples of food, beer, and camaraderie, opened the Cornelius Pass Roadhouse brewpub in the Imbrie house. After several more years and a battle to preserve the house and property from being razed, McMenamins purchased the rest of the property and stayed busy with renovations and additions. Along with the historic house from 1866, you'll find the 1859 granary barn (now containing a brass cognac still brought from France), the 1913 eight-sided barn, and the milk storage shed (now the Little White Shed pub, featuring a wood stove and cigars). The only "new" building is Imbrie Hall, the main bar and restaurant built with traditional barn-building techniques using wood gleaned from the old Henry Weinhard's brewery in Portland.

7.66 mi. At the stand of firs, turn right (if you end up at the apartments, you went the wrong way). Soon you come to a smartly constructed boardwalk that allows you to be in the middle of the wetland yet high and dry. Stay on the boardwalk at the next intersection.

7.97 mi. Turn left at the next large street, NW Cornell. Cross at NW John Olsen and continue on Rock Creek Trail.

8.34 mi. Right on NW Amberwood and left into Orchard Park, an official trailhead and parking lot for Rock Creek Trail. The playground has two fun fake rock climbing boulders with hand-holds. Take either trail at the fork—go left through the wetland and forest, or right through the nine-hole Frisbee disc golf course—both meet up downstream.

9.3 mi. Left on NW Wilkins.

9.56 mi. Right on NW 206th. Across the street, behind the chain link fence is a wheat field, the rich land for which the Tualatin Valley is famous. Don't blink as it may be gone next time you're here.

9.9 mi. Right on NW Quatama.

9.95 mi. Back to the start.

HOLLYWOOD, IRVINGTON, AND THE ALAMEDA RIDGE

AT THE TURN OF the nineteenth century, steamship captain William Irving was awarded a land grant bound by Tillamook and Fremont streets to the north and south, and 7th and 24th avenues to the west and east. Back then, this area was Portland's outer suburbs, far from the noise and squalor of downtown. Now, Irvington and the other neighborhoods this ride passes through are unquestionably inner, and getting a piece of property is decidedly not free.

Developers laid out neighborhoods and built opulent and grand homes for the businessmen who profited from Oregon's boom in natural resources in the early twentieth century. With plenty of skilled immigrant craftsmen hungry for work, the resulting homes are magnificent, as are the street trees and landscaping. Farther north, the same artisans built more modest houses, this time for themselves, the craftsmanship less opulent but no less solid.

Between rubbernecking beautiful homes, you'll glide through green parks, ride past pegged-jean-hipster cafes, and explore the storefronts of three stalwart shopping districts, where grandparents bring their children's children to shops they may have visited themselves as toddlers.

SCAVENGER HUNT

Bronze statues of Ramona Quimby, Henry Huggins, and Ribsy the dog

....

A weathervane shaped like a dolphin

....

A stethoscope bike rack

....

STARTING POINT

Hollywood/NE 42nd Avenue Transit Center (1410 NE 42nd Avenue)

9.86
miles

DISTANCE

EASY
148 feet

DIFFICULTY & ELEVATION GAIN

A STATUE OF BEVERLY CLEARY'S RAMONA QUIMBY

ROUTE ELEVATION

MAP KEY
— ROUTE
— NEIGHBORHOOD GREENWAYS
-- CAR FREE TRAIL
PARK/GREENSPACE
LANDMARKS

You'll find plenty to see in Hollywood's neighborhood center clustered around Sandy Boulevard. Unlike many other close-in neighborhoods, full of hip new stores and restaurants, Hollywood has held fast to its small town feel— complete with under-shopped antique stores and a soda fountain. But the un-hipness is too hip to stay secret; change is everywhere.

The namesake of the neighborhood is the Hollywood Theatre, built in 1926 in an ornate Spanish-Colonial style. Opened in the last days of silent film, it was the last theater in Portland to be designed for vaudeville performances including an orchestra and organ. As one of the only theaters outside of downtown with good streetcar access, it became very popular with the rapidly growing eastside population. But as entertainment choices increased, ticket revenues declined, and by 1975 the Hollywood divided its balcony into two 100-plus seat theaters, plus the original orchestra below which seats nearly 400. In 1997 a nonprofit purchased the theater and concentrated on returning it to a multi-use venue focusing on film. Today, the Hollywood shows 300 independent films a year, offers educational programs, and supports local filmmakers. One of its more quirky and fun partnerships is with Filmusik, a performance group of professional musicians, composers, and actors who screen classic and not-so-classic films to live music, dialog, and sound effects.

0.0 mi. Begin on NE 42nd with your back to the MAX train and bus mall and cross NE Halsey using the "road inductance sensor." (A fancy way to say: line up your bike on the pavement marking of a bicycle with a line through it and the traffic light will detect your presence and trigger the green light.)

0.13 mi. At NE Broadway, turn right and then left to stay on NE 42nd.

0.2 mi. Cross NE Sandy, taking in the new energy of the century-old Hollywood District . Three blocks to your right, between NE 44th and NE 45th, the Hollywood Farmers Market runs May to November every Saturday (the rest of the year on alternating Saturdays). Continue on NE 42nd.

0.52 mi. Left on NE Brazee.

0.83 mi. At NE 36th, enter Grant Park, which, along with the neighborhood and school, is named for President Ulysses S. Grant. (Although many of Portland's public high schools are named for presidents, at least Grant spent time near here: he was stationed at Fort Vancouver from 1852 to 1853.) Ride on the path past the school and swimming pool.

1.03 mi. Turn left at the tennis courts. The water fountain on the right features characters whose literary adventures happened on nearby Klickitat street; prolific novelist Beverly Cleary grew up in this neighborhood and used many of its sites in her children's books. Donations for the water fountain came from every state in the country. Continue around between the tennis courts and track, then turn right between the track and baseball field.

1.26 mi. Right onto NE US Grant.

1.55 mi. Left on NE 32nd and right on NE Tillamook.

2.07 mi. Left on NE 22nd.

2.24 mi. Right on NE Broadway. This main thoroughfare spans both sides of the river with thriving business districts in each quadrant it passes through. A streetcar line once ran on Broadway and many of today's shops are in the ornate 1920s storefronts where streetcar riders would do their shopping at day's end. Unlike many of Portland's shopping districts, Broadway has a bike lane so you can ride and scope out the shops in comfort and safety. A few blocks ahead and to the left is the Lloyd Center Mall. When built in 1960—at the expense of many original homes—it claimed to be the largest shopping mall in the world.

2.52 mi. Right on NE 17th, entering the gorgeous Irvington Historic District (the entire neighborhood is on the National Register of Historic Places).

2.82 mi. Use the sidewalk to bypass the dead end and turn right on NE Thompson. On the corner of NE 22nd is the Irvington Tennis Club's oldest building, built in 1905.

3.1 mi. Left on NE 27th.

3.85 mi. Left on NE Klickitat. At NE 15th, a block off the route to the right, is the vibrant shopping area along NE Fremont with a grocery store, library, cafes, restaurants. After crossing NE 14th, Klickitat turns into a car-free path. Enjoy the greenery of this hidden tunnel for just three and a half wonderful blocks until you enter leafy Irving Park. Ride between the ball fields and up the short steep hill.

4.8 mi. Turn right at the bathrooms and exit Irving Park carefully: the steep downhill path ends on busy NE Fremont. Cross Fremont and

2

Anybody who went to the University of Oregon or watches college football knows the name Autzen. Thomas J. Autzen was born in the soggy logging town of Hoquiam, Washington. In 1902, his Danish immigrant father purchased a wood products mill and 17-year-old Thomas began working in the company part-time doing cleanup and office work. In 1905 Portland held the Lewis and Clark Exposition to celebrate the 100th anniversary of the famous expedition. Over 2.5 million people thronged to Portland for the four-month fair that featured hundreds of exhibits from 21 countries. The mill management decided to make something new and unusual to demonstrate at the fair: a layered wood panel or "ply wood." A six-man "panel crew" brushed an animal glue—so odiferous they had to leave the room frequently—onto the layers of wood and used giant house jacks to hold the layers together. The whole process took an entire day to make just one set of panels. Young Tom Autzen was put in charge of showing off the panels, which turned out to be a sensation among fairgoers, particularly door manufacturers who saw great promise in the new technology, sparking a new industry in the northwest. The Autzens developed an automated process and within two years were able to make 420 panels a day. Today plywood is used in everything from houses to boats to designer furniture. The 54,000-seat (regularly cramming in 59,000) Autzen football stadium in Eugene was built in 1967 with a $250,000 donation by U of O alum Thomas E. Autzen, Thomas J's son. Ironically, Thomas J. Autzen went to Oregon State University.

continue straight on NE 9th. Pass a simple wooden church with a cornerstone — "Deutsche Congregationale Zion Kirche"—that hearkens back to the many German immigrants who started new lives in this neighborhood in the early 1900s.

5.34 mi. Right on NE Skidmore.

5.58 mi. At NE 14th turn right and then left to stay on Skidmore. Cross NE 15th carefully. A few blocks later, pass the Sabin HydroPark, which once had a fence around it and an enticingly off-limits lush green lawn. At the request of park-hungry local residents, the city took down the fence and turned it into the wonderful park, playground, and community garden you see today. The still-fenced-in set of machinery is a micro-hydro-turbine generator. It uses the pressure of the water as it leaves the tank to run a small generator that produces around 150,000 kilowatt hours per year (enough power for 13 houses).

6.12 mi. Right on NE 24th.

6.3 mi. Continue on 24th as it merges into NE Alameda. Taking up the entire triangular block on your left is the Tudor-style Autzen house built in 1927 for wood products company owner Thomas Autzen **2**. Here in the Alameda Ridge neighborhood, homes have soaring views to downtown and the West. Stuart Dr, just after the Autzen house, has some of the best views you can find without actually being inside a home. Stuart becomes a bustling sled hill on Portland's infrequent snow days.

6.58 mi. Alameda turns right on NE Hamblett, which turns back into Alameda after the two stop signs. Be careful crossing NE 33rd.

7.15 mi. Just after crossing NE 37th, turn right to stay on Alameda. Cross Fremont with care.

7.33 mi. Left on NE Klickitat.

7.49 mi. Cross NE 41st carefully and continue on quiet, peaceful Klickitat.

7.8 mi. Right on NE 47th.

8.1 mi. Right on NE Alameda.

8.31 mi. At 44th turn left to stay on Alameda.

8.41 mi. Go straight on NE Beaumont and turn left on NE 41st which becomes NE Wistaria. Here you descend back down the Alameda Ridge and return to Hollywood past more well-tended Craftsman homes and ultra-lush landscaping.

8.68 mi. Stay on Wistaria by turning left at 42nd and again at 43rd.

9 mi. Right on NE 47th.

9.45 mi. Right on NE Broadway.

9.71 mi. Left on NE 42nd. When crossing Halsey, notice the painted bike arrow directs you up on the sidewalk.

9.86 mi. Back to the start.

RIDE **9**

ALBERTA ARTS, CONCORDIA, AND WOODLAWN

King School Park

ORE ST

ND AVE

STARTING POINT
King School Park
(NE Going Street
and NE Grand
Avenue)

9.88
miles

DISTANCE

EASY
190 feet

**DIFFICULTY &
ELEVATION GAIN**

SCAVENGER
HUNT

Three murals on the pavement

································

Smiling Lego-head posts that keep cars from driving through a park

································

A combination bike rack, green roof, and stormwater rain garden

TRANSIT AND PARKING

TriMet bus 6 stops at NE Martin Luther King Boulevard and NE Wygant (or NE Prescott). Street parking is available on NE Going near the start.

THE ETHNICALLY DIVERSE Alberta District is a neighborhood in transition: churchgoers in their Sunday best on one block and a lawn covered with bike parts on another. It's also an area in which cyclists increasingly feel at home. Since 2000 this part of town has seen a huge increase in the number of people who choose biking as a way of life. These folks in turn have helped transform the neighborhood into the stuff comedians dream of. You'll experience plenty of real-life *Portlandia* on Alberta Street—especially if you time your ride to coincide with the Last Thursday Art Walk—with its ever-changing array of locally designed clothing, hipster bars, and off-beat eateries. Just off the main drag, the quiet neighborhood side streets, parks of soaring fir trees, and a linear arboretum provide a perfect balance to the bustle.

If you ride on a Sunday, May through November, the King Portland Farmers Market showcases fresh produce and locally made goods in the parking lot across the field from the start of the ride.

THE BRIDGE GOING THROUGH WOOD-LAWN PARK

1

The McMenamins Kennedy School, a 1915 elementary school that closed in 1975, is now a hotel with restaurants and bars, a soaking pool, brewery, and movie theater. This property has become a local favorite since reopening to the sound of the original school bell in 1997. The area surrounding this country school was originally several blocks past the end of the streetcar line, and a few blocks short of the city boundary. The first kids who attended the school lived in the surrounding countryside in homes without running water, sewer, electricity, or telephones. Today, it's just one of dozens of properties the McMenamin brothers have renovated into some of the most beloved landmarks in Oregon. Wander the hallways and peek into the school-themed bars—Detention, Honors, and Boiler Room—and admire the variety of artwork, which weaves in stories of the people who spent their days here, using their own photos, artifacts, and legends. The artists were instructed to stop when they were finished, and several of them, like the mosaic artist, just kept going and going, leaving us lots of whimsy and color to discover.

0.0 mi. From the starting point at King School Park, ride away from MLK Boulevard on NE Going. At NE 14th Place, one block to the right of the route (on NE Prescott), is a small group of delicious cafes, bars, and restaurants. If you visit, retrace your path and continue on Going.

1.5 mi. Use the cycle track to cross NE 33rd, and continue on Going for another block. Turn right on NE 34th.

1.78 mi. Left on NE Skidmore.

2 mi. Left on NE 37th. As you ride north consider a side trip to NE 42nd (five blocks to the right) with gems like Roses Ice Cream, serving milkshakes and burgers since 1950.

2.8 mi. Turn left on NE Simpson and ride until you reach NE 33rd and the McMenamins Kennedy School **1**. Explore the delightful former elementary school before retracing the route on Simpson back to 37th.

3.31 mi. Left on NE 37th. On your right is Fernhill Park. At 26 acres, the rolling hills and woods of the off-leash dog area is like a park in itself. Legend has it that before the land was acquired by the city in 1940, stolen cars were brought here, stripped, and then abandoned, resulting in an impromptu junk yard. Today, the most unsightly things is what a careless dog owner might have left behind.

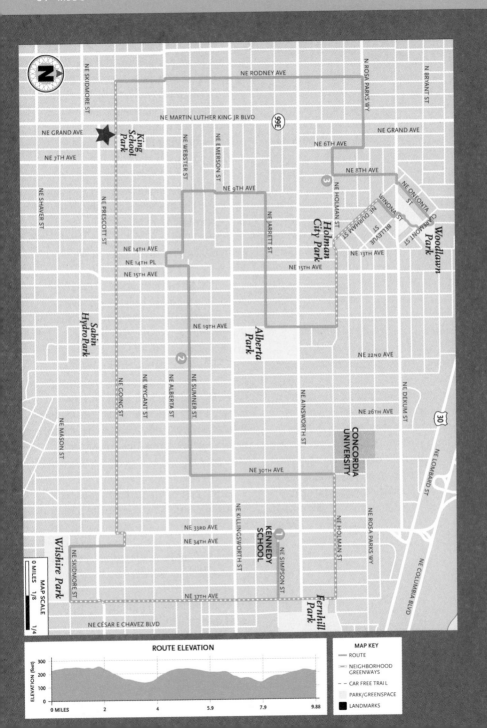

ROUTE ELEVATION

MAP KEY
— ROUTE
----- NEIGHBORHOOD GREENWAYS
- - CAR FREE TRAIL
PARK/GREENSPACE
LANDMARKS

2

Alberta is one of Portland's more famous revitalized neighborhoods thanks to its long stretch of brick-fronted streetcar-era shops filled with eclectic boutiques and restaurants. In the 1990s, artists began moving here, attracted by the cheap rent and gallery-ready storefronts, creating the "Alberta Arts District." Galleries spring up and disappear regularly, contributing to the do-it-yourself, counter-culture feel. Every month in the summer Alberta Street is closed to traffic between 15th and 30th for the Last Thursday Art Walk, when thousands of summer-hungry Portlanders pack the streets to stroll the galleries, gorge on treats from the street-side food vendors, listen to the bands and performance artists staged every few feet, and generally act weird, gawk, or both. Participation is intentionally unregulated (aside from the state-required food permits) so many small artists set up card tables and homemade stalls to sell their works and wares.

3.52 mi. Left on NE Holman. At the corner of NE 30th and Holman is Concordia University, nestled among the Craftsman cottages of the neighborhood that bears its name. Opened in 1905 to train pastors and school teachers, the private Christian institution added college classes in 1950.

4 mi. Left on NE 30th. The intersection with NE Killingsworth is a food lover's island in the middle of this quiet neighborhood. At least five acclaimed restaurants sit cheek to jowl here. Hungry? Take a culinary trip around the world without leaving the block.

4.58 mi. Right on quiet NE Sumner, running parallel to lively NE Alberta **2**. It's legal to ride on Alberta (as braver locals do), but without a bike lane, it's safer and more interesting to hitch your ride (there's at least seven bike corrals between 12th and 31st) and explore on foot. In less than a mile you'll find kitschy-cool clothing stores, galleries, brunch and ice cream spots, anarchist-youth-filled cafes, and an ever-changing array of food carts.

5.46 mi. Left on NE 14th Pl. Turn right on Alberta for a short block and then turn right on NE 14th Ave.

5.6 mi. Left on NE Webster.

5.79 mi. Right on NE 9th. Stay on 9th as it jogs right at NE Emerson. Two blocks later, cross busy NE Killingsworth carefully.

6.1 mi. Right on NE Jarrett.

6.6 mi. At NE 19th, Jarrett runs into Alberta Park. The park's magnificent Douglas fir trees are reminiscent of what stood throughout the neighborhood before pioneer settlers. Turn left on 19th.

6.75 mi. Cross NE Ainsworth. In this street's massive median and parking strips, the city, local residents, and the nonprofit Friends of Trees have planted more than 60 varieties of trees (including staghorn sumac, hackberry, and Kentucky coffee tree) to create the 2-mile-long Ainsworth Linear Arboretum.

6.9 mi. Left on NE Holman. At the intersection with 13th is tiny Holman City Park. Ride between the fun bollards placed here to block car traffic.

7.2 mi. Right on NE Durham.

7.45 mi. Right on NE Winona. Cross Dekum at the crosswalk, entering Woodlawn Park. Ride downhill through the park, go under the car bridge just after the playground, and turn left on the path toward the street sign for NE Oneonta.

7.75 mi. Left on NE Oneonta.

7.96 mi. Right on NE Dekum. The revitalized block before you contains all the elements of a cozy neighborhood center including a bakery, brewery, pizzeria, and a restaurant in an old firehouse. Check out the cool combination bike rack and rain gutter draining into a bioswale attached to Breakside Brewery (820 NE Dekum). This project is a partnership between the city and local artists to combine bike parking with a "green street" that diverts storm water runoff from rivers, channeling it to sidewalk plantings to filter out pollutants.

3

The Holman Street pavement mural at the intersection of NE 8th and NE Holman depicts the four seasons and neighborhood wildlife. Thought up by a local resident who wanted to bring the neighborhood together and get people interacting on their street, the mural was painted by 100 volunteers using $2000 in donations. The nonprofit City Repair organized this pavement mural along with others around Portland. The plaza-like feel helps slow down traffic and keep local kids safe.

7.99 mi. Left on NE 8th.

8.24 mi. Right on NE Holman and right on NE 6th. (Keep your eyes to the ground at the intersection of 8th and Holman **3**.)

8.45 mi. Left on NE Rosa Parks. Cross MLK Jr. Boulevard, which doubles as Highway 99 East. MLK has been stubbornly resistant to improvement over the decades, but new businesses worth investigating are springing up. Only the most courageous and life-weary cyclists dare ride on MLK so explore on foot if desired.

8.7 mi. Left on N Rodney. The block of Rodney between N Jarrett and N Jessup has so many big leaf maple trees it's like riding through a tree cathedral.

9.49 mi. At NE Alberta, turn left and then right to stay on Rodney.

9.68 mi. Left on NE Going. While upgrading Going to a neighborhood greenway, the city weighed the cost and traffic impact of various ways to get cyclists across MLK safely. The two striped crosswalks, concrete pass-throughs, and signs are the end result. Thanks to the courteous local drivers, most cars stop for bicycles here, but exercise caution regardless.

9.88 mi. Back to the start.

RIDE

10 HERITAGE TREE HUNT

STARTING POINT

Hollywood/Northeast 42nd Avenue Transit Center (1410 NE 42nd Avenue)

11.09
miles

DISTANCE

EASY
164 feet

DIFFICULTY & ELEVATION GAIN

A tombstone being eaten by a tree

....

A mural celebrating Cuban art and culture

....

Poetry post and art tree

....

TRANSIT AND PARKING

TriMet's MAX Red, Blue, or Green lines stop at the Hollywood/Northeast 42nd Avenue Transit Center as do TriMet buses 66, 75, and 77. Bus 12 stops on Sandy Blvd at NE 42nd. Look for street parking one block west of the MAX station on NE 41st and one block north on NE Broadway.

WITH AROUND 30 PERCENT of the city covered by 1.4 million trees, Portland is among the most tree-filled cities in the country. Forest Park, Hoyt Arboretum, and Tom McCall Waterfront Park, and others all figure large in Stumptown's greenscape. And the city's residential streets are brimming with tree treasures of their own.

Just a few pedal turns transport you from the starting point—an ultra-urban transit center with heavy traffic—to the quiet greenery and prosperous homes of the Laurelhurst neighborhood. Here you'll find the first of the 28 heritage trees on this 11-mile ride. The rest are scattered throughout eight other vibrant and bikable neighborhoods. To be "heritage," the Urban Forestry Commission must deem the tree significant for reasons of size (seven of the trees on this ride are over 100 feet tall; four are larger than 15 feet in circumference!) age, or historic or horticultural value. Since its conception in 1994, Portland's Heritage Tree program now includes more than 300 trees. Anyone can nominate a heritage tree (maybe you have one in mind?), and once the plaque has been put on, the tree can never be cut down.

Plan at least three hours to do this tour. The distance is relatively long, you'll be stopping a lot, and it can be challenging to quickly locate each tree. Consider this entire ride a scavenger hunt.

COLUMNAR INCENSE CEDAR
IN LONE FIR CEMETERY

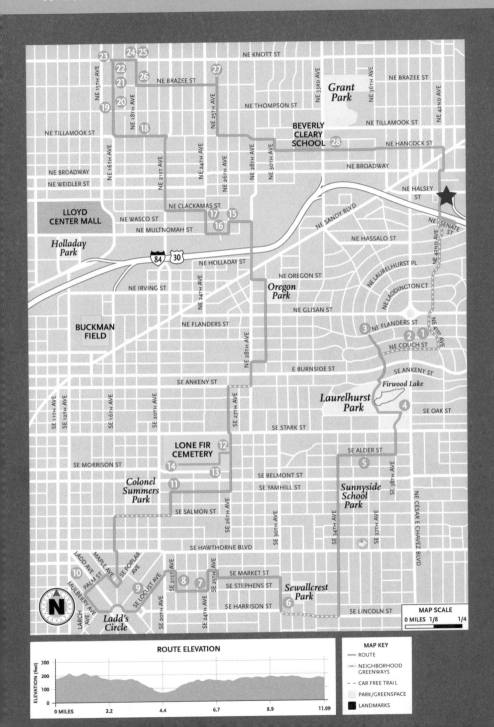

0.0 mi. Begin at the busy Hollywood/NE 42nd MAX station. Cross the pedestrian bridge to the south side of I-84. Make a U-turn at the bottom of the ramp on NE Senate and turn left on NE 42nd.

0.78 mi. Right on NE Couch. At 3945 is a Carolina poplar (*Populus* ×*canadensis*) **①**, a hybrid of eastern cottonwood and Lombardy poplar created in the 1830s. At 135 feet tall, this is the tallest tree on our tour. At the corner of Couch and NE César Chavez (on the same side of the street as the poplar) are two slender and graceful Japanese red pines (*Pinus densiflora*) **②**, which can grow more than 160 feet tall in their native Japan, China, and Korea.

1.04 mi. Turn right on NE Laurelhurst Pl to check out the monkey puzzle tree (*Araucaria araucana*) **③** at 415. Return the way you came on Laurelhurst and continue over E Burnside into Laurelhurst Park. The nearly 1000 trees in the park include Kentucky coffeetrees, ginkgos, grand firs, dawn redwoods, lindens, black oaks, sycamore maples, giant sequoias, white oaks, and around 100 conifers that are as old as 150 years. Make your way forward and left through the park to the path on the edge of SE Oak, then left (or however you like) to the horseshoe pits.

1.63 mi. Face the horseshoe pits and look (in the back and to the right) for the katsura tree (*Cercidiphyllum japonicum*) **④** which has heart-shaped leaves and smooth, white bark. This is the lone heritage tree in Laurelhurst Park. Leave the park by crossing SE Oak and continue into Laurelhurst Annex, built as a playground in 1911. Continue through this park and cross SE Stark on SE 38th (or cross busy Stark at the traffic light at SE César Chavez).

1.82 mi. Right on SE Alder. At 3652 is a Japanese maple (*Acer palmatum*) **⑤**, a common tree in Portland and planted worldwide for its beautiful fall foliage. Most Japanese maples are small and bush-like, but this large one has a full-fledged trunk.

2.07 mi. Left on SE 34th. Cross SE Belmont and then SE Hawthorne, two vibrant shopping districts and good places to stop for a refreshment or exploration.

2.75 mi. Right on SE Lincoln.

3.03 mi. Right on SE 30th. Across from the stately stone Mormon church, an impressive black walnut (*Juglans nigra*) ⑥ dominates the front yard at 1942 with its twisting, moss-covered branches and rough grey bark.

3.15 mi. Left on SE Market. At SE 25th, turn right and then left to stay on Market.

3.51 mi. Left on SE 24th and right on SE Stephens. At 1726 SE 24th is a western white pine (*Pinus monticola*) ⑦ —the state tree of Idaho, which can grow to more than 200 feet.

3.74 mi. Right on SE 21st. At 1816 is a London planetree (*Platanus ×acerifolia*) ⑧ with sloughing white bark and a warty trunk. Although this particular tree is only 60 feet tall, London planetrees can grow larger than 150 feet tall and 30 feet around.

3.85 mi. Turn left on SE Market, left on SE 20th, and right on SE Locust. Here you enter Ladd's Addition, home to four official rose test gardens. At 1836 is a Camperdown elm (*Ulmus glabra* 'Camperdownii') ⑨. This tree looks like a 1960s punk rocker when it bears a full "head" of leaves in summer; in winter its bare curly-cue branches look like the rocker after too much sex and drugs.

3.98 mi. Continue on Locust, past the east rose garden, and turn right on SE Harrison.

4.17 mi. Turn right into the central roundabout, go halfway around, and turn right to stay on Harrison.

4.31 mi. At the west rose garden turn right on SE Mulberry. The small tree (or large bush) at the corner of Mulberry and Larch (1905 SE Larch) is a ponticum rhododendron (*Rhododendron ponticum*) ⑩. Turn right on SE Palm (directly across from Larch). Watch for bikes crossing SE Ladd, this neighborhood greenway has one of the highest bike traffic counts in the city!

4.54 mi. Right on SE Maple. Ride counterclockwise around the north rose garden (two left turns) and continue on SE 16th. Use the conveniently placed button to trigger the pedestrian/bike crossing light at Hawthorne.

4.93 mi. Right on SE Salmon. On this neighborhood greenway, note the traffic circle designed to slow and discourage car traffic.

5.19 mi. Left on SE 21st and right on SE Yamhill. At 2104 is a river birch (*Betula nigra*) ⑪. Native to the eastern United States, Native Americans used its sap as a sweetener similar to maple syrup.

5.53 mi. Left on SE 26th. After crossing Morrison, pass DAWG Terrace on your right, a dog-friendly apartment complex boasting bike racks in the shape of unicycling dogs, fire hydrants on the front lawn, and of course, a dog house.

5.72 mi. Left into Lone Fir Cemetery, the oldest cemetery in Oregon, which had its first burial in 1846. About 10,000 of the 25,000 plots are unknown due to poor record keeping in the early years.

5.93 mi. Go straight ahead to the second intersection just before the flagpole and Civil War soldier statue on the right. On the left is the General Joseph Lane tree, a bigleaf maple (*Acer macrophyllum*) ⑫, named for Oregon's first territorial governor and first US senator. Big it is too, at 105 feet its crown has the largest spread of any on the tour. Continue straight ahead.

5.87 mi. Right at the T intersection. On the corner at the edge of the cemetery is Oregon's state tree, the Douglas fir (*Pseudotsuga menziesii*) ⑬. Lone Fir was named for this tree, back when it was the solitary fir tree on the property (this spook hotel is now home to more than 500 trees). Continue along the road on the edge of the cemetery. On the left is a columnar incense cedar (*Calocedrus decurrens*) ⑭, native to Baja, California, and at 110 feet, the second tallest heritage tree on this ride.

6.33 mi. After getting your fill of the many fascinatingly cool (or creepy) headstones, exit the cemetery (the same way you came in) and turn left on SE 26th. At Stark, turn left and then right to stay on 26th.

6.61 mi. Right on SE Ankeny and left on SE 28th. The intersection of 28th and Burnside is pretty busy. Walk on the sidewalk if you don't feel comfortable riding the block to Couch. This neighborhood is well stocked with places for a libation, snack, or both, plus a movie at the Laurelhurst Theater on the corner.

6.81 mi. Right on NE Couch and left on NE 29th.

7.23 mi. Left on NE Oregon and right on NE 28th. Continue on 28th across NE Sandy.

7.55 mi. Left on NE Wasco immediately after the I-84 overpass (the road doesn't go through; use the sidewalk). At 2607 look for a syca-more maple (*Acer pseudoplatanus*) 15 with pink-and-white-colored bark.

7.64 mi. Left on NE 26th and right on NE Multnomah. At 2517 are two large hedge maples (*Acer campestre*) 16. These are the lightweight boxers of the city's trees, with bulging, muscular trunks.

7.79 mi. Right on NE 24th. Just before NE Clackamas are two tulip trees (*Liriodendron tulipifera*) 17 on the right. These beauties are named for their tulip-shaped flowers.

7.89 mi. Left on NE Clackamas.

8.07 mi. Right on NE 21st (a busy street with no bike lane). Cross NE Weidler then cross NE Broadway: both have plentiful shops and restaurants to the left and right.

8.39 mi. Left on NE Tillamook. The house of George Earle Cham-berlain (governor and US senator in the early 1900s) is on the right at 1927. Behind the tall hedge is the thick rippled bark of a chestnut oak (*Quercus prinus*) 18 It's easiest to see the tree from the street or around the corner on NE 20th.

8.61 mi. Turn right on NE 16th and get ready for an onslaught of her-itage trees: nine in less than a mile. Irvington—developed from 1900 to 1930 as an exclusive suburb for wealthy citizens—isn't short of "normal" trees either. Hundreds line the streets here and shade the stunning houses.

Between the house and driveway of 1526 NE Thompson is a European white birch or silver birch (*Betula pendula*) ⑲. Just past the corner of Thompson on NE 16th (1529 NE Thompson) is a common horsechestnut (*Aesculus hippocastanum* 'Baumannii') ⑳. In the summer of 1993 a crazed bank robber drove straight into this tree after eluding police all day in a high-speed chase. Both driver and tree were undamaged but the car was totaled. (This story, thanks to Pedal Bike Tours guide Sam Haffner who watched the whole thing happen as an 11-year-old.)

On the corner of 16th and Brazee (1617 NE Brazee) is a slender and prehistoric looking dawn redwood (*Metasequoia glyptostroboides*) ㉑. At 2617 NE 16th are two big, beautiful American sweetgums (*Liquidambar styraciflua*) ㉒.

....

8.96 mi. From 16th, turn right on tree-packed NE Knott. At Knott and on both sides of the street between NE 14th and NE 17th you'll find a group of nine Caucasian wingnuts (*Pterocarya fraxinifolia*) ㉓, rare in Portland except for this cluster. The plaque is at 1408 NE Knott.

The house at 1719 NE Knott has two heritage trees. On the left is a Dutch elm (*Ulmus ×hollandiuca* 'Hollandica') ㉔. This elm is sick, you may notice dead branches in it. The city works closely with home owners to keep trees healthy, but many of these trees are at or beyond their normal lifespan. The tree with the massive trunk (the largest circumference on the tour, 20.88 feet) dominating the corner of the lot is a European or copper beech (*Fagus sylvatica* f. *purpurea*) ㉕ planted in 1916.

....

9.09 mi. Right on NE 18th. At 2546 is a huge example of the most common type of elm: a smoothleaf or field elm (*Ulmus minor*) ㉖. This one is busily devouring the curb. Its roots can extend for dozens of feet, under the street and into neighboring yards. Asphalt is more porous than concrete, and thus healthier for trees because it allows air to reach the roots.

....

9.19 mi. Left on NE Brazee.

....

9.55 mi. Left on NE 25th. At 2524 is an American sycamore (*Platanus occidentalis*) ㉗. Return the way you came back to Brazee and continue on NE 25th.

....

9.83 mi. Left on NE Tillamook.

10.09 mi. Right on NE 30th and left on NE Hancock. At 3331 is a European white elm (*Ulmus laevis*) ㉘. Like the field elm, several famous elders exist such as the "Elm of Bergemolo" in Piedmont, Italy, which is 200 years old and more than 18 feet around. Continue on Hancock.

10.87 mi. Right on NE 42nd. Cross NE Sandy, and continue around the S curve on 42nd.

11.09 mi. Cross NE Halsey and back to the start.

RIDE

11

ROSE CITY PARK AND ROCKY BUTTE

11.09
miles

EASY
174 feet

SCAVENGER HUNT

STARTING POINT

NE 60th MAX Station (NE 60th Avenue between Halsey and Glisan streets)

DISTANCE

DIFFICULTY & ELEVATION GAIN

A fence with metal images of dogs

··

An intersection mural with colorful geometric patterns

··

A park in the middle of the street

··

A statue of George Washington

··

TRANSIT AND PARKING

TriMet's MAX Blue, Red, and Green lines stop at the NE 60th station, as does TriMet bus 71. Street parking is available on NE 60th or side streets near the start.

ROAD NOTES About 3 miles into the ride, NE 92nd (for 0.6 miles after NE Thompson) has a fair amount of traffic and only a wide gravel shoulder. Ride carefully here and stay alert for

THIS RIDE TAKES YOU to the foot of Rocky Butte, one of Portland's tallest volcanoes, past a bar inside a jug, and along a ridge with stellar views of the city. You'll also find historic and walkable neighborhood centers including a vintage movie theater, an original soda fountain, and a brewpub. In between are lots of parks and unexpected sights like a side trip to a replica of a Michelangelo statue.

FAIRLEY'S PHARMACY

0.0 mi. From the starting point at the NE 60th MAX station, head north on 60th. This fairly busy street has no bike lane so consider riding or walking on the sidewalk the few blocks until the first turn.

0.13 mi. Left on NE Hassalo.

0.27 mi. Right on NE 57th. Erv Lind Stadium, within Normandale Park, is named for the improbable-sounding scenario of a local florist who also coached national title–winning women's softball teams.

0.35 mi. Turn left into the park via the path between the dog park and baseball backstop. This popular dog park beat out three other parks in an online contest to win a city-funded makeover. Continue on the path through the park and exit on Wasco.

0.55 mi. Right on NE 53rd.

0.93 mi. Right on NE Tillamook. On the left, after the intersection with NE 62nd, is Rose City Park, tacked on the corner of the golf course like an afterthought. This nice little park has a bathroom and water fountain, and a coyote or two are rumored to live in the thick brush on its slopes.

2.3 mi. Continue on Tillamook. At NE 81st the road narrows drastically: consider jumping onto the sidewalk for the next block. The giant building at 8000 NE Tillamook is the headquarters for Banfield Pet Hospital. Started here in 1955, the company now has 800 pet hospitals in the United States, Canada, Mexico, and Germany.

2.97 mi. Left on NE 92nd. On your right is Jason Lee Elementary, named for Oregon's first missionary and founder of Willamette University in Salem. He was partially responsible for creating the excitement over the Oregon Territories and the land grab that started the Oregon Trail. The road from NE Thompson for the next 0.6 miles has virtually no paved shoulder and a fair amount of traffic. You should be able to ride on the wide gravel shoulder but watch for potholes.

ROUTE ELEVATION

ELEVATION (feet)

400
300
200
100

0 MILES   2.2   4.4   6.7   8.9   11.09

MAP KEY

— ROUTE

∎∎∎ NEIGHBORHOOD GREENWAYS

– – CAR FREE TRAIL

▨ PARK/GREENSPACE

■ LANDMARKS

①

At the intersection of Sandy, 75th, and Beech sits a jug-shaped building. For this stop, leave the kids at home, or at the soda fountain up the street. Built in 1928 as a gas station and tire shop, today it's Pirate's Cove—an "adult" club and one of the best dive bars in America (according to *Maxim* magazine). Locals still refer to it as the Sandy Jug, a former name that just stuck. A few blocks away, the intersection of Sandy, Fremont, and 72nd has created a natural business hub. Fairley's Pharmacy has stood here since 1913 and still features a working pharmacy and soda fountain serving delicious ice cream and milkshakes, complete with wooden counter and bar stools. At the same intersection is a beloved doughnut shop, a bike shop, and the 1925 Roseway Theater—some might say the essential elements of modern culture.

3.21 mi. Steep NE Rocky Butte Road rises to the right and leads to 614-foot-tall Rocky Butte, one of the four volcanic cinder cones in Portland. If you're looking for some hill work, this would be an appropriate side trip (it's about a 500-foot climb). Joseph Wood Hill Park at the top is like a giant stone fortress with great views of southern Washington, the Columbia Gorge, and several mountain peaks.

3.7 mi. Left on NE Benjamin and left on NE Fremont.

3.83 mi. Right on NE 88th.

3.92 mi. Left on NE Beech. Within the tall trees to your right, behind the homes, lies the Grotto. This 62-acre Catholic shrine and heavily forested botanical garden is named for the cave at the base of a 110-foot cliff and contains a marble replica of Michelangelo's Pieta from St. Peter's Basilica in Rome. If you have time for a side trip and don't mind the steep downhill to the entrance, turn right on NE 82nd and right on NE Skidmore. Otherwise, continue on Beech.

4.29 mi. Cross 82nd carefully (use the stop light at Fremont, two blocks south, if you're having trouble getting a break in traffic). Continue on Beech, passing over the delightful intersection painting at 77th.

4.61 mi. At the intersection of Sandy, 75th, and Beech, look for a uniquely shaped building **①**. Sandy is very busy so cross carefully on Beech or go a block to the left and cross at the crosswalk.

4.84 mi. Right on NE 72nd. The Roseway Parkway, a wide grass median lined with trees, extends between Sandy and Prescott.

5.53 mi. Left on NE Alberta. Unlike the busy thorough-fare further west, Alberta is a neighborhood greenway here with bike-shaped sculptures topping the street signs. Large lots with yards full of fruit trees and gardens, combined with the lack of sidewalks, gives this street a country-like feel (dare I say back-woods at times).

5.94 mi. Cross NE Cully Boulevard. Here you can experience one of the best cycle tracks in Portland ❷.

6.8 mi. Left on NE 47th. The road rises gently all the way back up to NE Fremont.

7.58 mi. Cross Fremont. This is the heart of Beaumont Village, founded in 1910. Beaumont is home to a venerable bagel shop, a brewery, a longtime favorite burger restaurant, the last outpost of one of Portland's original coffee chains (Jim & Patty's), and at its far end, the Rose City Cemetery, along with much more. Ride on the street if you dare; walking on the sidewalk is safer. Continue on 47th.

8.02 mi. Left at the T intersection with NE Alameda. Notice how the houses have really moved into fancy mode, some flirting with mansion status.

8.48 mi. At NE 54th, a large church complex with palm trees and bamboo landscaping takes up several blocks. This is the SE Asian Vicariate and spiritual home to Portland's Vietnamese Catholics. Turn right into the parking lot to see a statue of St. Michael the Archangel with a map of Vietnam at his feet. At the back of the parking lot is a cool rock pinnacle featuring a demure Asian-featured Mary holding an Anglo Christ-child. Continue on Alameda.

❷

In 2011, what used to be a high-traffic road with crumbling edges and gravel "sidewalks" was given a $5.4M upgrade, and the cycle track was created. The fact that this expensive bike-centric infrastructure was placed in the blue-collar Cully neighborhood, rather than on a more high profile street, could be seen either as the city's desire to reach out to an under-served area, or an experiment to see if it will be successful in an out-of-the-way place. Regardless, it has turned a nasty road for bikes and pedestrians into a direct and safe showcase of active transit: a big win for bike lovers.

8.68 mi. Stay on Alameda as you cross the intersection with NE 57th and NE Sandy. The statue of George Washington (looking more than a little hipster-ish with tight knickers and biker socks) was donated to the city by serial statue donor Dr. Henry Waldo Coe in 1927. Coe is also responsible for the statues of Joan of Arc (in the Laurelhurst neighborhood), and Abraham Lincoln and Teddy Roosevelt (downtown).

8.95 mi. Right on NE 62nd.

9.08 mi. Left on NE Sacramento. The view from the ridge above the Rose City Golf Course is stellar, soak it up.

9.48 mi. Right at NE 72nd. At the bottom of the steep downhill (bike carefully), check out the public golf course's beautiful 1937 clubhouse on the right.

10.25 mi. Bear right on Broadway as 72nd ends. Just around the corner lies an Asian supermarket and restaurant complex with a multitude of exotic foods and low prices to match.

10.53 mi. Left on NE 62nd.

10.6 mi. At NE Halsey, turn right and cross the street to stay on 62nd. Halsey is very busy, has poor crossing opportunities, and the streets don't line up. Cross carefully here or detour a few blocks to the stoplight at 60th to cross.

10.85. Right on NE Hassalo. The bunker-like building as you turn the corner is, oddly enough, the Portland Rifle and Pistol Club. Turn left on NE 60th.

11.09 mi. Back to the start.

12 INNER NOPO'S HISTORIC AND HIP STREETS

NORTH PORTLAND, THE FIFTH, sometimes forgotten, quadrant, is fascinating and lively. This ride takes in panoramic views in the aptly named Overlook neighborhood, cruises past Craftsman cottages in Arbor Lodge, and explores the old shipbuilding and immigrant town of Albina (now uber-hip Mississippi Avenue and rapidly gentrifying Williams Avenue). Several of these neighborhoods have experienced the biggest swing in fortune of any in Portland. Families who've lived here for generations find themselves surrounded by a new wave of immigrants from all over the United States and beyond, attracted to Portland's down-to-earth art and music scenes, and quality of life reputation. Every new trip through this area finds buildings torn down and replaced with gleaming storefronts filled with an astonishing array of colorful and creatively outfitted new businesses—with patrons to match.

SCAVENGER HUNT

An intersection mural of a bicycle wheel, airplane propeller, and machinery

Six streets named for "M" states

Two bronze sea turtles

STARTING POINT

Overlook Park MAX Station (3698 N Interstate Avenue)

10.19
miles

DISTANCE

EASY
194 feet

DIFFICULTY & ELEVATION GAIN

TRANSIT AND PARKING

MAX Yellow Line stops at the Overlook Park station. No close bus service. Street parking is available on Interstate Ave and side streets.

OVERLOOK HOUSE

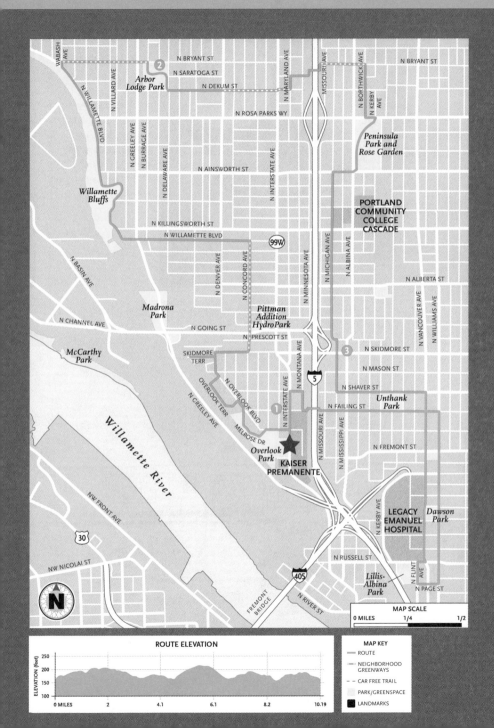

N BRYANT ST
N SARATOGA ST
N DEKUM ST
N BRYANT ST

WABASH AVE
N WILLARD AVE
N VILLARD AVE

Arbor Lodge Park

N MARYLAND AVE
MISSOURI AVE
N BORTHWICK AVE
N KERBY AVE

Peninsula Park and Rose Garden

N ROSA PARKS WY

N GREELEY AVE
N BURRAGE AVE
N DELAWARE AVE

N AINSWORTH ST

N INTERSTATE AVE

Willamette Bluffs

PORTLAND COMMUNITY COLLEGE CASCADE

N KILLINGSWORTH ST

N ALBERTA ST

N WILLAMETTE BLVD

99W

N BASIN AVE

N DENVER AVE
N CONCORD AVE
N MINNESOTA AVE
N MICHIGAN AVE
N ALBINA AVE
N VANCOUVER AVE
N WILLIAMS AVE

Madrona Park

N CHANNEL AVE

N GOING ST

Pittman Addition HydroPark

N PRESCOTT ST

McCarthy Park

SKIDMORE TERR

N SKIDMORE ST
N MASON ST
N SHAVER ST

Unthank Park

3

OVERLOOK TERR
N OVERLOOK BLVD
N CREELEY AVE
MELROSE DR

N INTERSTATE AVE
N MONTANA AVE
I-5

N FAILING ST

1

Willamette River

Overlook Park

KAISER PREMANENTE

N MISSOURI AVE
N MISSISSIPPI AVE

N FREMONT ST

N KERBY AVE
N FLINT AVE

LEGACY EMANUEL HOSPITAL

Dawson Park

NW FRONT AVE

30

N RUSSELL ST

NW NICOLAI ST

405

Lillis-Albina Park

N PAGE ST

FREMONT BRIDGE

N RIVER ST

MAP SCALE

0 MILES   1/4   1/2

N

MAP KEY

— ROUTE

--- NEIGHBORHOOD GREENWAYS

- - CAR FREE TRAIL

▨ PARK/GREENSPACE

■ LANDMARKS

ROUTE ELEVATION

ELEVATION (feet)

250
200
150
100

0 MILES   2   4.1   6.1   8.2   10.19

1 ──────────── ────────────

Interstate Avenue, also known as Highway 99 West, was the main road north to Vancouver before I-5 was built and still has many motels with fabulous original neon signs. Through the years, Interstate became a local thoroughfare, the neighborhood deteriorated, and the motels became very dated (one motel advertises "TV") and are now of dubious quality. Partially to combat this urban blight, TriMet built the Yellow Line in 2004. It was originally intended to run from Milwaukie to Vancouver, but because it was just approved by voters in Portland, only the section to the Columbia River was built. Today with construction cranes busy all along Interstate and condos and restaurants popping up, a new feeling of revitalization and excitement is in the air.

0.0 mi. Begin at the Overlook Park MAX station, ride north on N Interstate **1**, and take your first left on N Overlook Blvd. Overlook Park has the first of many killer views of the West Hills, the Willamette River, downtown Portland, and the Union Pacific Rail Yards below. To visit it, you can either make your way down the grassy slope bordering N Overlook or go back to N Interstate and turn right. Retrace your steps/revolutions to continue the route.

0.21 mi. Left on N Melrose. At 3839 is the Tudor-style Overlook House, built in 1927 by the civic-minded owners of a creamery, and donated to the city in 1951. If you like (and it's not busy with a wedding), go around back and check out the lush landscaping on the cliff's edge.

0.38 mi. Left on N Overlook Blvd and left on N Overlook Terr.

0.7 mi. Left on N Overlook Blvd.

0.8 mi. Left on N Skidmore Terr. This lush street dead-ends at Mocks Crest Property, also known as Skidmore Bluffs, a secret (shh!) local favorite for sunset picnics under the oaks. Return the way you came and turn left back onto N Overlook.

1.08 mi. Right on N Skidmore.

1.25 mi. Left on N Concord. In one block, get on the left sidewalk to ride up, around, and onto the Going Street overpass, then back down again. Wasn't that fun? Continue on N Concord.

1.8 mi. Left on N Willamette.

2.35 mi. Cross N Greeley. If you're not comfortable crossing busy Greeley here, go one block to the right and cross at N Killingsworth—by the food cart pod—then continue straight until you reach N Willamette and turn right to rejoin the route.

2.6 mi. As Willamette arcs right, and then sharply left, there's a nice overlook of the Willamette Escarpment, also known as Willamette Bluffs. Below you can see Swan Island, home to Portland's first airport in the late 1920s and Henry Kaiser's shipyards around World War II. Today it's a major industrial area. The grassy bowl below is a popular unofficial dog park.

3.11 mi. At the T intersection with N Rosa Parks, turn left to stay on Willamette.

3.41 mi. Right on N Wabash then immediately right on N Bryant.

3.84 mi. After crossing Greeley, cut diagonally through Arbor Lodge Park (stop for restrooms and water here if needed, and check out Harper's Playground ❷ while you're at it). Exit at the intersection of Delaware and Dekum.

4 mi. Left on N Dekum.

4.7 mi. Left onto N Maryland and right on N Saratoga. Follow Saratoga as it becomes the Bryant Street Overpass and crosses I-5.

5.09 mi. Right on N Borthwick.

5.14 mi. Cross N Rosa Parks and turn right into Peninsula Park. This gem of a park has the oldest rose garden in Portland (it turned 100 in 2013). Due to budget cutbacks, the garden had fallen into disrepair and the roses were suffering, but 3000 disease-resistant plants

❷

In the middle of Arbor Lodge Park is the very awesome Harper's Playground, named for a young lady whose physical disabilities made it impossible for her to use the former playground. After extensive renovations, it's now designed to be used by all, including disabled children, and has been adopted by big-hearted donors, including The Timbers Army, Portland's professional soccer team fan club. Today, Harper's Playground includes a hand-crank-operated waterfall, climbing walls, and a number of brass animal statues.

3 ───────────────────

In 2009, the corner of Mississippi and N Skidmore was transformed from a weed-choked lot with a demolition-worthy garage into a gleaming hall of Victorian architecture with a bar that's packed most nights of the week. In place of weeds, food carts have sprung up, surrounding the bar with stomach-pleasing delights. Mississippi as a whole has undergone the most striking transformation of almost any neighborhood in Portland. It's a good-news bad-news story. With its proximity to the rail and ship yards and industrial jobs along the river, this has always been an immigrant neighborhood. However, from the 1950s through the 1980s, racial prejudice, the closing of the street car lines (including the Mississippi Line), the demolition of Albina's downtown core, and the arrival of L.A.'s Crips and Bloods gangs, caused many residents to move out, and this area had the highest number of abandoned buildings in the city. Compare that bleak picture with the prosperous and tragically hip scene before you. Today, gang violence is much less common, but as the rents have skyrocketed, many of the law-abiding, longtime, and long-suffering residents of the neighborhood have been pushed out.

were donated and put in the ground in time for the anniversary. Ride on the path to the opposite side of the park. When you get there, stop and smell the roses if they're in bloom; otherwise just marvel at the beautiful sunken garden layout and fountain.

5.66 mi. Right on N Ainsworth.

5.77 mi. Left on N Michigan Ave. Where Michigan crosses Killingsworth is a vibrant if historically troubled street with an odd assortment of furniture shops, student-oriented cafes and restaurants, hipster bars, and markets whose revenue is based on the unholy trinity of energy drinks, beer, and cigarettes. The Cascade campus of ever-expanding Portland Community College is two blocks to your left; across the street is Jefferson High School, home of the "Demos" (Democrats).

6.33 mi. As Michigan bends left and becomes N Prescott, turn right to stay on Michigan. At the intersection of Michigan and Skidmore, you are just one block west of the thirst-and-hunger-quenching food cart pod, Mississippi Marketplace **3**. Continue down low-traffic Michigan or hop over to lively Mississippi.

6.8 mi. Left on N Shaver. In one block cross busy N Mississippi (unless you're already on it; if so rejoin the route here).

7.03 mi. Continue on Shaver, passing Unthank Park on your right. The park was named for Dr. DeNorval Unthank, a local champion of minority rights for fifty years beginning in 1929, only three years after Oregonians amended the constitution to allow African Americans to settle here permanently. The large building in the park is home to Self Enhancement Inc., which helps at-risk youth realize their potential.

7.24 mi. Right on N Vancouver. The downtown-bound half of the N Williams/N Vancouver corridor has one of the highest bike traffic counts in Portland—more than 6500 per day.

8 mi. Right on N Russell and left on N Flint. Lillis-Albina Park has a great downtown view from the basketball court.

8.13 mi. Left on N Page and left on N Williams.

8.54 mi. Continue up Williams. The ornate copper bandstand roof in the corner of Dawson Park is all that's left of the cupola of a grand building that once marked downtown Albina. At the low point of discrimination and urban decay in this neighborhood, the land where the building stood—on the corner of Williams and Russell—was sold to Emmanuel Hospital. The Williams corridor epitomizes the huge transformation these neighborhoods have experienced. Once an Oregon Food Bank warehouse, the HUB Building on the corner of Williams and Failing is now an urban mall filled with hip shops and restaurants.

9.03 mi. Left onto N Failing.

9.61 mi. After crossing Mississippi again, wind up the ramp of the Failing Street Bridge, cross over Interstate 5, and continue on Failing.

9.8 mi. Right on N Montana and left on N Shaver.

9.93 mi. Left on N Interstate.

10.19 mi. Back to the start.

KENTON, ST. JOHNS, AND PENINSULA VIEWS

STARTING POINT
Kenton/N Denver Ave MAX Station (8399 N Interstate Avenue)

10.97 miles

DISTANCE

EASY 177 feet

DIFFICULTY & ELEVATION GAIN

An aluminum windmill sculpture called Whirlymajig

A street painting of trees through the seasons

TRANSIT AND PARKING

TriMet's MAX Yellow Line stops at the Kenton/N Denver station. TriMet bus 4 stops at the corner of N Kilpatrick and N Denver. Parking is available on the street.

THERE ARE FEW BETTER PLACES to start off a blue-collar-themed ride than Kenton, Portland's bedroom community for the area's early twentieth century meatpacking district, which lay just over the bridge to the north. Neighboring St. Johns occupies the tip of the peninsula formed by the Willamette and Columbia rivers and is very much a river town. But it's easy to forget that, if only because there isn't much access to either river if you don't have a badge for a port facility. In the 1850s, these rivers meant captains of industry could build factories, shipping terminals, and railroads to utilize and export Oregon's collected natural riches, creating lots of jobs in the process. The pollution that came along with the industry is a major skeleton in Portland's greener-than-thou closet. Today, despite economic difficulties, Oregon is a leading exporter in the country, and St. Johns sits right in the middle of the action.

You'll be exploring the neighborhoods settled by the immigrants attracted here by the river, warehouse, and railroad jobs. You'll also get glimpses of the Willamette River and the industries that line it, at least what's left of them. You'll glide through historic commercial districts, parks lined with 1960s apartment buildings, and view the gothic arches of Portland's most awe-striking bridge. Time your ride right and you can catch Kenton Third Thursday when neighbors and businesses get together for art, music, and food.

ST. JOHNS
BRIDGE

The proud symbol of Kenton, the 31-foot-tall Paul Bunyan statue was built in 1959 to celebrate Oregon's 100th birthday—as well as Oregon's tradition of rugged pioneer individualism and its then-main economic driver, the timber industry. The mythical logger weighs 6 tons and was crafted by Kenton Machine Works from welded steel and plaster. Paul's face was supposedly made by a welder named Frenchy, who would call the owner of the Machine Works from various bars to back up his artistic claims to other bar patrons. Today the statue is on the National Register of Historic Places for its qualities as "novelty architecture."

0.0 mi. Begin at the Kenton/N Denver Ave MAX station and cross Interstate for a close-up of the Paul Bunyan statue ❶.

0.05 mi. Cross Denver, turn right on N Willis and enter Kenton Park. Given the sheer abundance of parks in Portland, not all can be standouts. Many are merely awesome. Kenton is one of these: boring, wonderful old green grass, trees, playgrounds, ball fields, and bathrooms. Ride through the park and exit at N Delaware.

0.38 mi. Right on Delaware and left on N Argyle.

0.68 mi. Right on N Peninsular and left on N Hunt.

1 mi. Right on N Hamlin. At the end of the block go through the bike- and pedestrian-only concrete barrier and turn left on N Houghton. Stay on Houghton as it curves to the right and becomes N Alaska.

You'll pass University Park, which used to be the name for the entire neighborhood back when the university *was* the entire neighborhood. The park's Charles Jordan Community Center, named for Portland's first African American City Commissioner, was built in the early 1940s as part of a gigantic federal housing project for the thousands of workers who moved here to work in the shipyards during World War II.

1.65 mi. Stay on Alaska as it becomes N Trenton, and enter the New Columbia community where hundreds of barracks-style buildings once housed shipyard workers, and after the war became Columbia Villa, a public housing complex. By the 1990s, the buildings were aging, the infrastructure inadequate, and the 1,300 low-income residents physically, socially, and economically isolated from the community. Crime was rampant, demands for change equally so. In 2001, the community received $151 million in funds and was completely rebuilt to become New Columbia, the beautiful model community of 854 affordable housing units that you see before you.

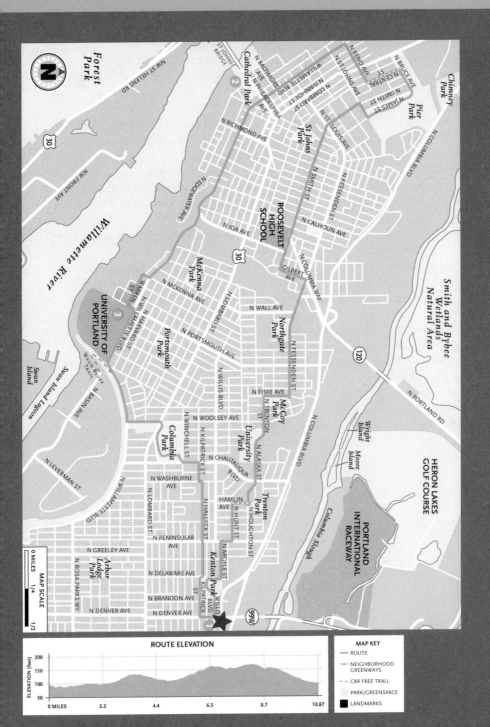

ROUTE ELEVATION

MAP KEY

— ROUTE

▱ NEIGHBORHOOD GREENWAYS

– – CAR FREE TRAIL

PARK/GREENSPACE

■ LANDMARKS

1.9 mi. Right on N Fiske.

2.07 mi. Left on N Fessenden.

2.69 mi. Cross a bridge over a gaping chasm known simply as "the cut." Just over a mile long and up to 90 feet deep, the St. Johns railroad cut was built in the early 1900s to allow trains access to the Willamette River from the Columbia.

2.85 mi. Where N Fessenden intersects with N Columbia Way, take a sharp left onto N Gilbert (use the crosswalk).

3.10 mi. Right on N Smith. A few blocks later, pass the back side of Roosevelt High School with its Colonial Revival bell tower.

3.42 mi. Continue on Smith. The impressive Spanish Colonial church at N Calhoun was built in 1921 as the Assumption Catholic Church. When the archdiocese consolidated four parishes, this beautiful site became Assumption Village, low-cost assisted living for seniors, which was in short supply and high demand. The goal is to provide "public square"-oriented living for seniors with opportunities to interact with each other and the community.

4.07 mi. Cross N Saint Louis and stay on Smith.

4.47 mi. Right on N St. Johns. One block past N James, turn left on the path into Pier Park (on unmarked N Pier Park Place), where acres of fir trees dwarf the picnic tables. It's fun to ride up and down the rolling hills of the dirt paths and pretend you're doing some serious mountain biking. The path exits the park on Bruce.

4.83 mi. Left on N Bruce.

5 mi. Left on N Central.

5.24 mi. Right on N Reno. A few blocks later cross Lombard—carefully.

5.55 mi. Left on N Willamette. At the intersection of Willamette and Catlin is the Your Inn Tavern, out of place in this residential neighborhood. The sign says it has been around since 1923, and the barman, who happened to be enjoying a cigarette in the doorway, invited us in with a hearty "best burger in town!"

6.1 mi. At N Baltimore you'll get your first view of the exceptionally cool St. Johns Bridge ❷. The grassy area under the bridge is lovely, uniquely situated Cathedral Park. Look for the spot where the pointed gothic arches of the bridge supports line up perfectly, one inside the next. If you'd like to ride across the bridge (and back) turn left on N Philadelphia directly before the bridge and then U-turn right on the bridge sidewalk. Rejoin the route on Willamette.

6.21 mi. Continue on Willamette. Few places in Portland feel more like a rural Oregon town than downtown St. Johns. A few blocks to the left of the route on N Lombard is the St. Johns Theater & Pub, one of the last remaining buildings from the 1905 Lewis and Clark Exposition. It was moved here downriver by barge after the expo and is now part of the McMenamins enterprise.

6.87 mi. Still on Willamette, pass the Portway Tavern (with friendly, crusty bar staff, and a big beautiful maple on the back patio) and look for N Edgewater on the right. For a short side trip, follow the steep downhill that leads through the forest and a gate to the riverbank, thick with cottonwood trees and highly toxic superfund sites. North Portland Greenway, a group of active transportation and recreation supporters, is working to get a multi-use path constructed that would pass right through here on its way from the Eastbank Esplanade to Kelley Point Park.

7.17 mi. Stay on Willamette and re-cross the cut.

❷

The 1931 St. Johns Bridge connects directly into Forest Park on the other side of the Willamette River and is named for its two cathedral-like towers with gothic arches. The last bridge on the Willamette, it is one of only three suspension bridges in Oregon. Given the distance from downtown, it took a lot to convince the city to replace the original ferry here with a bridge, but it ended up being built during the Great Depression, providing jobs for many local residents. The bridge is also rumored to be haunted. In 1949 Morris Leland abducted 15-year-old Thelma Taylor, held her under the bridge (before Cathedral Park was built), and murdered her there. On dark nights they say you can still hear her screaming for help . . .

❸

Today's University of Portland started in 1891 after a chancellor at Salem's Willamette University defected, bringing many faculty members and students with him to form Portland University. It closed in 1900 and was reopened, with support from Indiana's Notre Dame University, as Columbia University (oddly enough since it sits above the Willamette, miles from the Columbia River). Aside from high academic standards, the University of Portland is well known for its women's soccer program, which won national championships in 2002 and 2005.

7.72 mi. Right on N McKenna. Where McKenna turns left and becomes N Warren, you'll see a nice park with the Student Led Unity Garden (SLUG), an indicator that we're on the edge of the University of Portland. ❸

8.01 mi. Left on N Portsmouth and right on N Willamette. As Willamette turns sharply left to follow the edge of the bluff, enjoy the views of downtown Portland and the Fremont Bridge. At Willamette and Harvard is the Waud Bluff Trail. This ramp and stairway down to Swan Island was long dreamed of by bicycle activists as it cuts out miles of detours for those wanting to access the island from the north.

8.91 mi. Left on N Woolsey. Columbia Park Annex has an excellent view of the West Hills, downtown, the Portland Harbor industrial area, and the river itself. Next door (At 4333 N Willamette) is the Victorian John Mock House built in 1894.

9.12 mi. Cross N Lombard and turn right into Columbia Park, home to the fairytale Columbia Cottage, built in 1940 and now rentable for private events. Ride either direction diagonally through the park, ending up on N Winchell and N Chautauqua.

9.5 mi. Left on N Chautauqua.

9.66 mi. Right on N Kilpatrick.

9.78 mi. Left on N Washburn and right on N Halleck.

10.45 mi. Stay on Halleck as it becomes Kilpatrick and pass Kenton Park.

10.75 mi. Left on N Denver and right on N Interstate.

10.87 mi. Back to the start.

14

LAKES, WETLANDS, AND KELLEY POINT PARK

WHAT COULD A PORT MOVING hundreds of thousands of containers per year—filled with everything from pantyhose to cars—possibly have in common with one of the largest urban wetlands in the United States? The answer: they sit right next door to each other.

For thousands of years water has been the cheapest way to move goods. Today, the Columbia River and the lower reach of the Willamette River, are still major economic drivers of the local economy, exporting the largest volume of wheat in the United States and importing the third highest number of cars, among other products.

Begin the tour at the former site of the second largest city in the state (Vanport City) and ride along a levee above a raceway born on its deserted streets. You'll ride between a major—and majorly polluted—waterway and alongside a fragrant yet vital facility keeping our natural waterways pollution-free. After riding along Smith and Bybee lakes and the giant cranes of the port, you'll end up at Kelley Point Park before returning along the waterfront with its swift current, houseboats, and gently rusting derelict ships.

SCAVENGER HUNT

A sculpture of a beaver skull

....

The place where the Willamette and Columbia rivers meet

....

STARTING POINT

Delta Park/Vanport MAX Station (N Expo Road and Victory Boulevard)

14.7 miles

DISTANCE

MODERATE
184 feet

DIFFICULTY & ELEVATION GAIN

TRANSIT AND PARKING

TriMet's MAX Yellow Line stops at the Delta Park/Vanport station. There's no bus service here. Free parking is available across N Expo on N Burrage at the Vanport Wetlands.

THE CONFLUENCE OF THE WILLAMETTE AND COLUMBIA IN KELLEY POINT PARK

1

The story of Vanport began when merchant ship builder Henry Kaiser ramped up Portland's shipbuilding industry to aid the effort during World War II. His three "emergency" shipyards built Liberty ships—cheap, quick-to-assemble cargo ships with an intended life span of only five years—to replace ships sunk by German U-boats. Together the yards on Swan Island, St. Johns, and Vancouver built 455 Liberty ships (one in less than five days) of the 2700 constructed nationwide between 1941 and 1945.

To fill all those jobs, Kaiser recruited laborers from across the country. This influx of workers meant a need for housing, and in 1943 the community of Vanport was founded along a stretch of Columbia River lowlands around 15 feet below river level. With 40,000 people, Vanport became Oregon's second largest city and the largest public housing project in the country. About 40 percent of the workers were African American who had just moved to a state with a very racist past: charges of segregation and racism were rampant. After the war ended, the population of Vanport dropped to just over 18,000 and Vanport College was built to educate returning soldiers.

Then, over a rainy Memorial Day weekend in 1948, the dike holding back the Columbia River collapsed, flooding the town. Some residents were away for the holiday and the flood waters rose over about 30 minutes, but 15 people still lost their lives that day and Vanport was completely destroyed. Many of the displaced were forced to seek shelter in extremely crowded conditions in today's Mississippi and Alberta districts, where overt discrimination limited opportunities for decades.

After the flood, all that was left of Vanport City were the paved streets and foundations of the buildings. It was the perfect place for a drag strip, and in 1961 an official race was held during the Rose Festival, complete with the hazards of colliding with these concrete ruins or ending up in one of the marshy lakes. This perfect combination of thrill and danger is how Portland International Raceway was born.

The Columbia Slough runs parallel to the Columbia River for about 19 miles, eventually emptying into the Willamette River. This creek is actually the remnant of an original slough and wetlands that once covered about 50 square miles. As the area developed in the early 1900s, the wetland was drained and beginning in 1910, city sewage was piped directly into the slough. Stockyards, dairies, trucking, freight, and wood products companies all dumped their waste in the slough, making it one of Oregon's most polluted waterways. Eventually it got so nasty that lumber mill workers refused to handle logs that had been stored in its water. Finally a sewage treatment plant was built in 1952 and the city stopped waste from being thrown and pumped into it. You probably won't want to swim in it, but you'll see lots of ducks and great blue heron fishing for dinner in its muddy waters, along with deer, beaver, otters, and up to 150 species of birds.

0.0 mi. From the MAX Delta Park/Vanport station turn left on N Expo. This is the former location of Vanport City **①**: site of a tragic event in Portland's history.

0.47 mi. At the sign marked "Schmeer Rd." Make a U-turn to the right onto the side road, then left on the Columbia Slough Trail **②** that runs along the levee which keeps the slough from overrunning its banks.

2.33 mi. Continue following the path as it goes under the railroad tracks and turns right becoming the Peninsula Crossing Trail, a tranquil **3.5** mile path that runs parallel to N Portland Road and links the Willamette and Columbia rivers.

2.95 mi. Left at the sign marked "Kelley Point Park." Cross N Portland and follow the path as it goes between the concrete barriers. This road, closed to cars, leads along the northern edge of the Smith and Bybee Wetlands Natural Area, an urban 2000-acre freshwater wetland.

Soon you'll come to a canoe launch from where boaters can enjoy a completely natural experience surrounded by the city. A short hike will lead you down to the brushy shore of Smith Lake. (Watch out for mosquitoes, they love it here.)

4 mi. Just as the road exits the park, you'll pass Interlakes Trail on the left. For a side trip on foot, you can follow the trail for almost a mile onto the peninsula between the lakes and into the world of beaver, bald eagles, cottonwood, and alder. (Did I mention the mosquitoes?)

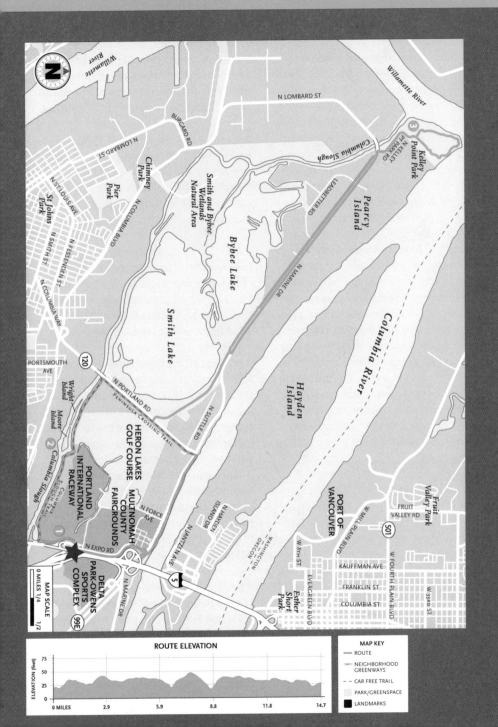

③

Secluded, green, and full of river smells and towering black cottonwood trees, Kelley Point Park sits at the confluence of the Willamette and Columbia rivers. Named for Hall Kelley, an early supporter of emigration to the Oregon Territory, the park looks significantly different than it must have originally. It was once an island, called Pearcy Island, separated from the mainland by Pearcy Slough and owned by the Port of Portland. The port dumped material dredged from the rivers to build the surrounding terminals here and filled in the slough until the island was connected to the peninsula. The city acquired the land in 1984 and did a nice job of adding just enough amenities for ease of access while still preserving the nature of the 104-acre park.

Turn left on N Marine and stay on the multi-use path. The Port of Portland's 416-acre Terminal 6 on the right receives ships twice as long as the 35-story US Bancorp Tower is tall. Look left as you ride along the path and you may spot the top of the St. Johns Bridge against the West Hills beyond.

6.37 mi. Turn right onto the road at a post marked "40 Mile Loop End" and take the first right into Kelley Point Park **③** (on Kelley Point Park Road). On your left is a canoe launch at the end of the Columbia Slough. You'll pass several parking lots; stay on this main road until it dead ends at the last parking lot.

7.13 mi. At the farthest parking lot, turn left and ride into the park on the asphalt path. Across from the bathroom is a short dirt path; this is a good place to go down and see the Columbia River and her tugboats and barges. Continue on the main path, which winds counterclockwise around the peninsula.

7.55 mi. To find the point where our dear Willamette is swallowed up by the mighty Columbia, look for a huge rolling green lawn on your left and two benches with a historical plaque on your right. Even the overlook is partially obscured by two trees. It's unassuming and unspectacular, no wonder Lewis and Clark missed it both times they paddled by. However, what it lacks in grandiosity, it makes up for with a complete absence of roads, machinery, or other signs of human impact. This wonderfully natural place is a respectable end for a river so abused by people through the decades. From the path, there are several beach access points to the Willamette River on the right.

8.1 mi. Turn left at the Y intersection. In a few yards the trail will end at a parking lot (the first one you passed on the way in; next to a well shot up interpretive sign). Turn right on Kelley Point Park Road.

8.63 mi. Turn left on N Marine and get back on the car-free path.

11.01 mi. Stay right at the Y intersection to re-enter Smith and Bybee Wetlands Natural Area.

12.1 mi. Cross N Portland and turn left on the Peninsula Crossing Trail.

12.65 mi. Cross N Marine and turn right on the multi-use path next to the river. Along the near shore, the steel tugboat Jean—built in 1938 to tow logs and push barges loaded with wood chips and paper products—is moored without her twin paddle wheels. On your right is the Expo Center.

13.83 mi. Cross N Marine at the light (an unmarked freeway intersection before I-5) and ride on the opposite sidewalk to the MAX Expo Center station. Continue past the MAX station on the path.

On your right, across the street, the fenced-in, 90.5-acre Vanport Wetlands offers habitat for more than 100 species of birds, as well as amphibians and mammals, including beaver, coyote, and deer. As beautiful and natural as it looks now, it's been pretty heavily worked on to get rid of invasive plants and increase water flow to more closely mimic the natural hydrology in order to invite more birds. Unfortunately, aside from a leash-free dog park across from the MAX station, there are no public paths.

14.7 mi. Back to the start.

THE COLUMBIA CROSSING AND VANCOUVER

STARTING POINT

Expo Center MAX Station (near N Expo Road and Marine Drive)

10.55
miles

DISTANCE

MODERATE
230 feet

DIFFICULTY & ELEVATION GAIN

SCAVENGER HUNT

A totem pole shaped like a beaver

....

A statue of a girl handing a man a flower

....

TRANSIT AND PARKING

Transit and parking: TriMet's MAX Yellow Line stops at the Expo Center station. You can park in the Portland Exposition Center parking lot for free (or $8 when an event is going on).

THE ONLY RIDE TO LEAVE Oregon takes us to the oldest settlement in the Northwest, Fort Vancouver, and the city that sprang up around it: Vancouver, Washington. Portland's "little brother" is rich in history and not far behind when it comes to bicycle infrastructure, or at least it's far ahead of much of the rest of the United States. This ride will take us across the Columbia River—"the great river of the west"—to a riverfront with great views, a replica of the fur trading fort that was the seed of the Northwest and Oregon Trail, a lush college campus named for the explorer William Clark, and through Vancouver's inner city neighborhoods and historic and revitalized downtown.

MANSION ON OFFICERS
ROW, FORT VANCOUVER

The Portland Expo Center was originally built as livestock exhibition halls to serve the meat processing plants of the North Portland Stockyards located between here and the Kenton neighborhood. But in 1942 it housed 3,500 Japanese-Americans from Oregon and Washington as part of an Executive Order to prevent them—many of whom were US citizens—from possibly aiding Japan in the war effort. Families were forced to live in the livestock pens for five months before being sent off to internment camps in Idaho and California. The Torii Gate, with replica identification tags for each person interred here, was put up to commemorate this abuse of civil liberties. On the MAX platform, a sculpture of a steamer trunk represents the sum total of possessions that Japanese-American families—many of whom owned homes, buildings, and businesses—were allowed to bring.

0.0 mi. Begin the ride where the tracks end on the Expo Center ❶ MAX platform. Ride up the winding path to the sidewalk on NE Marine and turn right.

0.12 mi. At the corner of N Marine Dr and the freeway entrance for I-5 north, go left across the crosswalk and ride on the bike path following all signs marked "Vancouver."

0.42 mi. Turn right at the intersection with the sign toward "Vancouver." Go through the tunnel and ride up onto the I-5 bridge, crossing a channel of the Columbia River (the North Portland Harbor) to Hayden Island. Notice the houseboat community below you, an interesting mix of neat and tidy with some real flotsam. With its prime location in the middle of the Columbia River, just across from Fort Vancouver, Hayden Island has undergone many name changes by its discoverers, re-discoverers, and owners. Previous names include Menzies Island, Image Canoe Island, Vancouver Island, and Shaw Island; Hayden Island comes from Gay Hayden, the American who claimed the island as his donation land claim in 1851.

1.1 mi. Cross at the crosswalk (N Tomahawk), stay on the sidewalk.

1.23 mi. Cross N Hayden Island Drive and turn left using the crosswalk button.

1.28 mi. Turn left at the bike path intersection towards Vancouver and enjoy the ride across the Columbia River ❷, the second largest river in the country. Reserve some attention for the narrow bike path and ignore the smell of exhaust and the layer of grime it leaves on the metal struts.

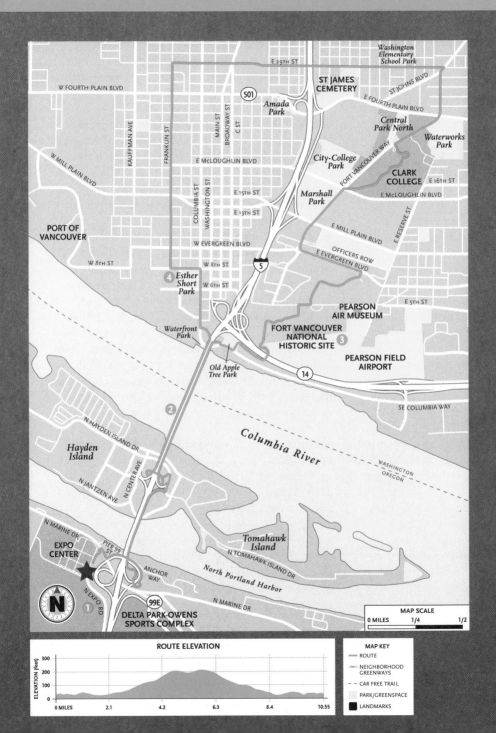

2

How lucky are you to be biking rather than driving across the Columbia River? The experience of the roiling water beneath, the sight of tugs, barges, sail, and fishing boats, the green banks of the two states receding into the distance, and the mountains in the background is pretty cool. This is actually two bridges: the northbound bridge was built in 1917 to replace the overworked ferry, the southbound bridge was added in 1958. The original bridge charged a toll of 5 cents for each horse and rider or automobile and had an electric streetcar. Both the toll and streetcar ended in 1940 when the two states purchased the bridge. The big steel towers are vertical lift decks that rise to let through ships up to 176 feet high. This happens 10 to 20 times a month, much to the chagrin of drivers (about 130,000 each day). Due to the age of the bridges and their importance to interstate commerce and the tens of thousands of commuters, plans have been afoot to replace the bridges. The number of lanes, the cost, whether it will include light rail, and the possibility of tolling have all been heavily fought over for years. At least no one is contesting the presence of bike lanes.

2.18 mi. After the crossing, the path curves around to SE Columbia. Turn left onto the Columbia River Renaissance Trail (at the sign marked "Waterfront Trail") which runs from downtown Vancouver eastward five miles to Wintler Park, passing shops, restaurants, and parks, all with sweet views of the working river. Our route takes us a different direction so save this exploration for another day (or what the heck, ride a portion, or all of it, now and come back).

2.25 mi. Turn left at the sign marked "Fort Vancouver." This short path dead ends between the freeways at the oldest apple tree west of the Mississippi, planted in 1826. The little tree has survived floods, loss of limb, the 1962 Columbus Day storm, the building of Highway 14, and its own predicted 50-to-70-year life span. You can get a cutting from the tree during The Old Apple Tree Festival on the first Saturday in October every year.

Turn right and ride up the ramp onto the Vancouver Land Bridge, one of the Confluence Project's seven art installations along the river that "reflect the people and environment of the Columbia River basin." Created by Maya Lin, the renowned architectural designer and artist best known for creating the stirring Vietnam Veterans Memorial in Washington D.C, this is certainly the coolest freeway crossing I've ever seen. Keep your eyes on the skies and you might catch a small airplane dropping in for a landing at Pearson Field.

2.50 mi. Follow the curving bridge over Highway 14 and back down (nice how the thick native vegetation of the ramp obscures the freeway). Leaving the bridge, we arrive at the birthplace of the Northwest as we know it today: Fort Vancouver ❸.

2.99 mi. Turn right when the path dead-ends at (unmarked) E 5th.

3.06 mi. Left on the unmarked road with the sign "Visitor Center." To the left is Vancouver Barracks, a US Army post from 1849 until its decommissioning in 2011. At the top of the field is the museum, bookstore, and visitor center.

3.38 mi. Left on the path next to E Evergreen. This line of houses is Officers Row, housing for Vancouver Barracks officers and their families. Some of these stately beauties date back to 1850 and several are named for famous inhabitants, such as Ulysses S. Grant and George C. Marshall. When restoration began in the mid-1980s a shortsighted city official referred to them as "21 white elephants nose to tail." Now, they're the city's pride and joy.

3.78 mi. Right at the roundabout onto Fort Vancouver.

4.19 mi. Cross E McLoughlin and turn right onto the bike path to enter the Clark College campus. The 100 cherry trees on the campus of this two-year school were given to the City of Vancouver by a Japanese company to commemorate the

❸

Now a National Historic Site, Fort Vancouver's reconstructed buildings make for a fun afternoon of exploring. After taking over John Jacob Astor's disastrous fur-trading settlement in Astoria in 1824, Dr. John McLoughlin (rival fur trader for the Canadian Hudson's Bay Company) decided to move the operation upstream to escape the massive amounts of rainfall at the mouth of the Columbia. Situated in an Eden of mild weather—with plentiful water, abundant natural resources, access to the ocean, and unsurpassed agricultural land—Fort Vancouver quickly became the center of civilization in the area. Reachable only by an arduous six-month sea voyage, or an equally long, unexplored and dangerous trek overland, the fort was famous for its civilized comforts and hospitality. Contrary to his orders to give no Americans assistance, McLoughlin freely loaned desperately needed food and clothing to thousands of Oregon Trail pioneers, and sent them to the rich farmland of the Willamette Valley, thus earning himself the title "Father of Oregon."

4

Esther Short Park is the oldest public square in Washington, donated by Esther herself in 1853 out of her and her late husband's donation land claim. Vancouver's version of Portland's Pioneer Courthouse Square has undergone a similar transformation. Vancouver's downtown has drastically revitalized since the dark days of neglect and abandonment. The story goes that the mayor was hit in the back with a shopping cart and threatened by a territorial transient during a "take back the park" event in 1997. Sentiment to revitalize the park took off after that, and today you'll find a beautiful space with a basalt riverlike fountain (including misters for summertime frolicking) and a clock tower donated by the owner of Burgerville.

100th anniversary of Washington's statehood in 1889, and every April the college hosts a Sakura (cherry blossom) Festival under the falling blossoms. Walk or ride slowly through campus on the path before coming to a dead end at the Gaiser Hall Student Center and Cannell Library.

4.64 mi. Turn left at the library, take your first right on Fort Vancouver, and ride down the hill. At the intersection with 4th Plain is a Burgerville. This quintessential Oregon burger chain actually hails from Vancouver (since 1961) and is still headquartered here today. It's one of the greenest quick-service restaurants around, composting its food waste, using 100 percent wind power, offering free-range beef, and using only trans-fat free canola oil that it recycles into biodiesel. Best of all, Burgerville welcomes bicyclists at its drive up windows! Continue on Fort Vancouver.

5.23 mi. Turn right on St. Johns and then left on E 29th, a long, quiet, pleasant stretch for biking. As you cross I-5 (the highest elevation of the ride) look south for a nice view of downtown Portland in the distance.

6.73 mi. Left on Franklin.

7.81 mi. Left on W 8th. Esther Short Park **4**, on your right, is the oldest public square in Washington.

8 mi. Right on Columbia.

8.28 mi. Just after the railroad bridge with the interesting war-themed murals, turn left onto the Columbia River Bridge. (Follow the sign for "I-5 Bike Path Portland.")

9.18 mi. Turn right at the bottom of the bridge; follow all signs marked "Max Station." Across the road, the Jantzen Beach Supercenter occupies the former site (from 1928 to 1970) of the 123-acre Jantzen Beach Amusement Park

("Coney Island of the West") and named for an investor, the owner of Portland's own Jantzen Swimsuit company. Ride through the tunnel.

9.27 mi. Turn left toward N Hayden Island and cross at the crosswalk, then turn right and cross the street and continue on the sidewalk.

9.42 mi. At N Tomahawk cross in the crosswalk and continue on the bike path over North Portland Harbor.

10.10 mi. Turn left at the path intersection toward "MAX Station."

10.4 mi. Cross N Marine, turn right on the sidewalk and left onto the winding path to the Expo Center Max station.

10.55 mi. Back to the start.

WILLAMETTE RIVER PATHWAYS

ARTING POINT
Skidmore Fountain
MAX Station (1st
Avenue under the
Burnside Bridge)

11
miles

DISTANCE

EASY
174 feet

**DIFFICULTY &
ELEVATION GAIN**

SCAVENGER HUNT

A half-submerged
submarine in the
Willamette River

....

A mural of a great
blue heron, osprey,
and other birds

....

A sculpture of
a beaver

....

TRANSIT AND PARKING

TriMet's MAX Red and Blue lines stop at the Skidmore Fountain
station. TriMet buses 12, 19, and 20 stop at SW 2nd and W Burnside, and several other lines stop at the bus mall on SW 5th and
SW 6th. Look for street parking with long enough meter time or
park in any of the numerous pay lots.

ROAD NOTES The old Sellwood Bridge—the new and improved
one is slated to open in 2015—has a treacherously narrow
sidewalk that bikes and pedestrians must share. Ride carefully

THIS CLASSIC LOOP ALONG both sides of the Willamette River takes you from the heart of the historic center of Portland across two bridges—among the oldest and newest in the city—to restored natural areas on former industrial land. You'll tour the various and impressive efforts the city has made to transform areas once ruled by heavy industry in an age when the river was considered only a convenient place to dispose of unwanted chemicals and manufacturing and construction waste. The three-mile, nearly traffic light–free spin on the Springwater Corridor to Sellwood seems like a quiet pastoral river scene, but in reality it's the lifeblood of the metropolis. A few of Portland's famous attractions are found throughout the ride: a landfill turned bird-filled oasis, a historic amusement park, and a gondola whisking medical students, patients, and tourists between the hospital on the hill (built in 1919) and the futuristic new buildings on the water.

OAKS PIONEER CHURCH
IN SELLWOOD

What is now the Oregon Museum of Science and Industry (OMSI) started in the early 1900s as a collection of odd artifacts in the hallways of City Hall. When it was evicted from there it moved first to a hotel, then a house (with a planetarium on the front lawn) until getting its own purpose-built building in Washington Park (now the Portland Children's Museum). It has been at its current site, an old power plant under the Marquam Bridge, since 1992. Older kids love the interactive science experiments, puzzles, and games, and of course there's a toddler play area. The museum also has an IMAX theater, planetarium, and laser Floyd (songs from rock band Pink Floyd set to lasers in the planetarium): classic.

0.0 mi. Begin at the Skidmore Fountain MAX station and walk your bike south on 1st for half a block and then turn left on SW Ankeny. Cross SW Naito, entering Governor Tom McCall Waterfront Park, and turn left on the path along the river.

0.4 mi. Continue following the path as it turns right and crosses the Steel Bridge.

0.6 mi. Turn right at the end of the bridge onto the Vera Katz Eastbank Esplanade. This 1.5-mile pathway, created with great effort, is among the most popular biking stretches in the city. Follow the ramp down and across the 1200-foot-long floating walkway.

1 mi. At the top of the floating walkway, turn right to continue on the Eastbank Esplanade. Ride cautiously—beware the tight corner and pedestrians—as you approach the Oregon Museum of Science and Industry ❶. Down on the water, the USS Blueback was the last non-nuclear submarine to join the navy, in 1959, and the last to be decommissioned, in 1990.

2.2 mi. Follow the path as it turns left and becomes SE Caruthers.

2.4 mi. Right on SE 4th. The Springwater Corridor begins ahead (a prominent gateway sign is above the path entrance). The gateway is almost symbolic of your entry to an entirely different place. As the cliff rises to your left, the river opens up on the right and the city sounds drop away.

2.6 mi. After passing under the Ross Island Bridge you'll see Ross Island itself, 400 acres in the middle of the Willamette River. Most of Ross Island is owned by Ross Island Sand and Gravel, which mined gravel there from 1926 to 2001. But 45 acres on the north end is the Ross Island Natural Area, home to at least fifty species of birds including osprey, eagles, and heron.

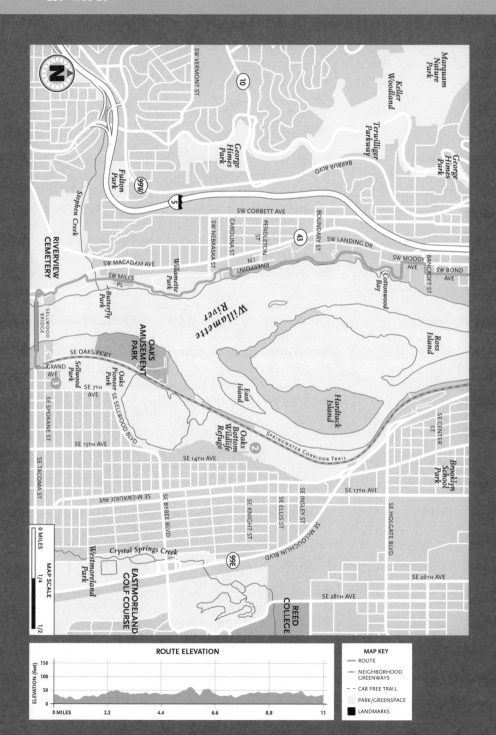

ROUTE ELEVATION

MAP KEY
— ROUTE
— NEIGHBORHOOD GREENWAYS
-- CAR FREE TRAIL
▨ PARK/GREENSPACE
■ LANDMARKS

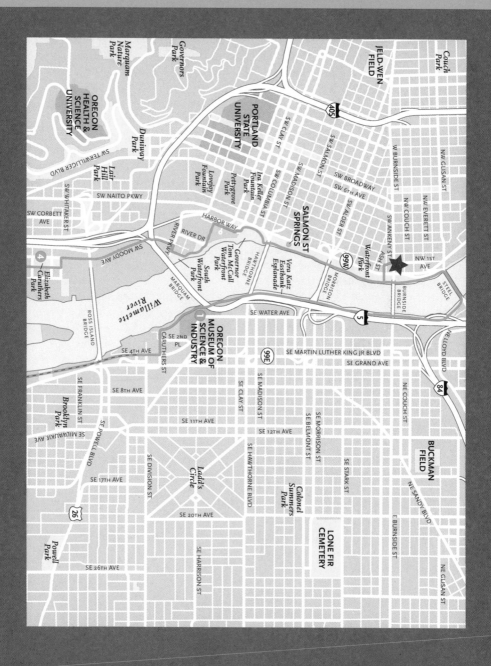

4.2 mi. Still on the path, pass Oaks Bottom Wildlife Refuge ②, a 141-acre wetland city park and the last remaining natural area on the lower Willamette. On the bluff to the left, the beautiful mural of birds found in the wetland is on the side of Wilhelm's Portland Memorial Funeral Home.

4.9 mi. Ride by Oaks Amusement Park Skating Rink ("Healthful Exercise, Delightful Pleasure"). Opened in 1905, an attraction timed to accompany the Lewis and Clark Centennial Exposition, for decades this was the main attraction along the Springwater Corridor—back when a train ran on it instead of joggers. The 1948 flood put the park underwater for a month and destroyed most of the rides as well as the old-growth wood floor of the roller skating rink. The rink was rebuilt on top of airtight steel drums, which luckily floated as planned when it endured two more floods in 1964 and 1996. Even with today's modern distractions, the park still draws families and mini-golfers in the summer, and roller-skaters year-round.

5.4 mi. Left on SE Spokane. Small, wooden Oaks Pioneer Church ③, on the corner of Grand and Spokane, looks straight out of a picture book but has a streak of wanderlust.

5.5 mi. Take your next right on unmarked SE Grand (follow the sign for "SW Portland"). Then turn right on unmarked SE Tacoma and ride across the Sellwood

②

The Oaks Bottom Wildlife Refuge is one of the last remaining examples of how the banks of the Willamette were before industrialization: wet, green, and full of life. Like the rest of the east bank, this area became a convenient place to dump garbage and excess debris from things like freeway construction. The city bought it in 1969 to prevent it from being developed as industrial land and planned to fill it in for recreation uses. Groups like the Audubon Society spoke up and in 1988 it became Portland's first wildlife refuge, a welcome new beginning. Then, in 2004 it was made the city's first migratory bird park, with thousands of birds (at least 185 species) stopping off for a snack and a rest on their annual north-south trips. Today, Portland Parks & Recreation works to mimic the water levels of the wetland as if it were fully connected to the surrounding watershed by increasing and decreasing the water flow at a dam near the trail.

3

Oaks Pioneer Church was built in 1851 upriver on the outskirts of the town of Milwaukie and moved twice and remodeled twice during the first hundred years of its life. By 1960, it was slated to be torn down. The local neighborhood association (curiously, local to Sellwood rather than the church's native Milwaukie) raised $4,300 at the last minute to have the church barged downriver to its current location; further contributions of time, money, and furniture brought it back to tiptop shape. Now the church's elegant stained glass windows (with an inscription: "Presented by the bible class 1889") witness around 400 weddings a year.

Bridge. Built in 1925, this frankenbridge is the only crossing of the Willamette within more than 10 miles and has the highest traffic of any two-lane bridge in Oregon. Unfortunately, the old bridge has only a three-foot-wide sidewalk—and only on one side—making it awkward, if not dangerous, for bikes and pedestrians. When cracks were discovered in 2004, the county decided it had to be replaced. The new bridge, slated to open in 2015, will have a 12-foot walkway for pedestrians, and a 6.5-foot bike lane on both sides: a huge improvement.

5.9 mi. Turn right after the bridge onto the bike path. Along the west side of the river you'll see signs for the Willamette Greenway, an unsung hero in the Oregon land use pantheon. The 1973 Willamette River Greenway Act requires that public access, native vegetation, and scenic views be considered when planning new development along the river.

6.3 mi. Turn right and then left at bike signs marked "SW Portland/Downtown." As the path traverses the South Portland Riverbank, you'll pass a group of houseboats at the Willamette Moorage; a crossing of Stephens Creek, which serves as habitat for native salmon, trout, and eel; and 1-acre Butterfly Park, developed with the mission to turn a "derelict patch of land" into a tiny but "biologically productive" greenspace.

6.6 mi. Continue straight into Willamette Park. Stay on the path closest to the river and enjoy the sights and smells of its green banks.

7.1 mi. Turn right as the path ends on the road (unmarked SW Beaver), just before the Willamette Sailing Club. Follow the path as it winds around condos and office buildings. Take your time riding this quiet and peaceful stretch: the speed limit here is 10 mph.

8.3 mi. Turn sharply right as the path ends on unmarked SW Moody.

8.5 mi. Turn right on SW Bancroft and left on SW Bond. The distinctive blue tile–roofed building ahead of you is the flagship and headquarters of the Old Spaghetti Factory. Navy veteran Gus Dussin started the company in 1969 in downtown Portland, and today their hand-made Italian food is served in 40 locations in the western United States. This location, built in 1984, with 500 seats, great river views, and "antique bric-a-brac," holds the hearts of many Portlanders.

8.83 mi. Turn left on SW Whitaker at the Oregon Health & Science University (OHSU) Center For Health and Healing ❹. Turn right on SW Moody and follow the bike path left across SW Moody to the cycle track, passing under the Portland Aerial Tram. The impressive two-way bike and pedestrian cycle track (separated and raised above the street) runs for the next half mile and represents the future of bicycle infrastructure in the city.

9.2 mi. Here the cycle track passes under the MAX Orange Line on its way to the west end of the Portland-Milwaukie Light Rail Bridge, due to be completed in 2015. This car-free crossing (the first bridge to be built on the Willamette since 1973) will carry TriMet's MAX lines, buses, and the Portland Streetcar. Bicyclists and pedestrians will enjoy generous 14-foot-wide walkways.

❹ Completed in 2006, the OHSU Center for Health and Healing is LEED Platinum (the highest energy efficiency rating possible) and is the largest health care facility in the United States to get the top rating. It's served by the Portland Aerial Tram which connects the upper and lower campuses, holds 75 passengers, and takes three minutes to make the journey. The tram is bike friendly and the views from the top are unbeatable.

9.4 mi. Cross SW Moody under the I-405 overpass using the bike-activated crossing light and following the bike-specific pavement markings across the streetcar tracks. Isn't it nice to feel like a legitimate part of the city traffic system?

9.6 mi. Turn right on SW River and left on the crosswalk (at the round-about) in front of the Marriott Hotel. On your left is RiverPlace, the first redevelopment of industrial land along the river. Completed in 1995, it includes 700 apartments and condos, office and retail space, and more than 300 hotel rooms.

9.8 mi. Left on SW Montgomery.

10 mi. Right on SW Harbor Way.

10.1 mi. Turn left on the waterfront path and re-enter Tom McCall Waterfront Park.

10.9 mi. Turn left before the Burnside Bridge (between the fountain and the Saturday Market Pavilion). Cross SW Naito and ride across Ankeny Plaza with its white cast iron arches and Skidmore fountain.

11 mi. Back to the start.

17 HAWTHORNE DISTRICT AND THE INNER EASTSIDE

MIGHT AS WELL CALL THIS the "heart of bike-friendly Portland ride." Once decaying no-go zones, the inner southeast neighborhoods led the charge back into the city and are reaping the quality-of-life benefits. On this tour you'll explore several neighborhood greenways, neighborhoods with some of the city's best restaurants, one of Portland's acknowledged "upscale" neighborhoods, as well as the crunchy ex-ghetto now known for bikeability and good living. You'll see a maze of beautiful houses, giant trees and rose gardens, and more fantastic shops, cafes, and restaurants than you can visit in a month of Sundays.

SCAVENGER HUNT

Two bikes mounted on two different poles

....

A chimney with a smile made out of stones

....

A winged monster made from bike parts

....

STARTING POINT

Skidmore Fountain
MAX Station (1st
Avenue under the
Burnside Bridge)

DISTANCE

9.15 miles

DIFFICULTY & ELEVATION GAIN

MODERATE 226 feet

TRANSIT AND PARKING

TriMet's MAX Red and Blue lines stop at the Skidmore Fountain station. TriMet buses 12, 19, and 20 stop at SW 2nd and W Burnside, and several other lines stop on SW 5th and SW 6th. Look for street parking with long enough meter time or park in any of the numerous pay lots.

FIRWOOD LAKE IN LAURELHURST PARK

SW NAITO PKWY

SW 1ST AVE

NW 2ND AVE

South Waterfront Park

Governor Tom McCall Waterfront Park

Vera Katz Eastbank Esplanade

MARQUAM BRIDGE

HAWTHORNE BRIDGE

MORRISON BRIDGE

BURNSIDE BRIDGE

STEEL BRIDGE

ASH ST

SW

99W

1

Willamette River

ROSS ISLAND BRIDGE

SE WATER AVE

5

OREGON CONVENTION CENTER

SE 3RD AVE

SE GRAND AVE

MARTIN LUTHER KING JR BLVD

SE 6TH AVE

NE DAVIS ST

NE COUCH ST

99E

SE 7TH AVE

84

30

NE LLOYD BLVD

26

SE POWELL BLVD

SE CLAY ST

SE 11TH AVE

SE 12TH AVE

BUCKMAN FIELD

SE 17TH AVE

SE ELLIOTT AVE

Ladd's Circle

SE MADISON ST

SE MORRISON ST

SE STARK ST

SE ANKENY ST

NE SANDY BLVD

NE IRVING ST

SE LADD AVE

Colonel Summers Park

LONE FIR CEMETERY

E BURNSIDE ST

3

SE 21ST AVE

SE 20TH AVE

SE HARRISON ST

SE HAWTHORNE BLVD

SE SALMON ST

NE GLISAN ST

SE 26TH AVE

2

Piccolo Park

SE CLINTON ST

SE DIVISION ST

Sewallcrest Park

SE YAMHILL ST

SE BELMONT ST

SE PINE ST

NE 28TH AVE

Oregon Park

NE 32ND AVE

SE 31ST AVE

Sunnyside School Park

SE WASHINGTON ST

SE 33RD AVE

NE FLANDERS ST

NE ROYAL CT

Coe Circle

NE LADDINGTON CT

SE LINCOLN ST

SE 34TH AVE

Laurelhurst Park

Firwood Lake

SE ANKENY ST

NE COUCH ST

SE CESAR E CHAVEZ BLVD

SE 41ST AVE

0 MILES   1/4   1/2

MAP SCALE

ROUTE ELEVATION

ELEVATION (feet)					
300					
200					
100					
0					

0 MILES   1.8   3.7   5.5   7.3   9.15

MAP KEY

— ROUTE

⋯ NEIGHBORHOOD GREENWAYS

- - CAR FREE TRAIL

▢ PARK/GREENSPACE

■ LANDMARKS

1

Active until 1917, the USS Oregon was at the cutting edge of technology when she was built in 1896, with her coal-powered boiler doing 16 knots (about 18 mph). When the word hit that the USS Maine had exploded in Havana, she immediately set out on the trip around the horn of South America en route to Cuba, making the journey in just over two months. This feat was heavily covered in newspapers, first, because it was an astonishingly fast trip, and second, it pointed out the importance of building the Panama Canal—the United States couldn't afford to spend two months sending a ship from the Pacific to the Atlantic. At the base of the monument, a time capsule was sealed up on Independence Day 1976, to be opened in 2076.

The Oregon Maritime Museum is housed inside the sternwheeler steam-powered tugboat "Portland." She was the last one built in the United States in 1947, retired in 1981, and today is the last one operational in the country. She's a reminder of the days when the river was full of such boats, back when this spot was the city's port and full of the comings and goings of ships, sailors, loggers, farmers, and longshoremen handling cargo destined for delivery all over the world.

0.0 mi. Begin downtown at the Skidmore Fountain MAX station and walk your bike south on 1st, away from the Burnside Bridge. Turn left on SW Ankeny, cross SW Naito into Waterfront Park, and turn right on the path. As you ride alongside the river, look for the towering mast of the USS Oregon, and down on the water, the tugboat containing the Oregon Maritime Museum **1**.

0.7 mi. Turn right after crossing under the Hawthorne Bridge and right again on the bridge's entrance ramp. Ride across the bridge.

1.53 mi. At the foot of the bridge, cross unbikable SE Grand and continue on Hawthorne. At SE 12th lies Cartopia, one of the city's original food cart pods featuring such taste delights as crepes, Belgian-style fries in a cone, po' boys, and whatever cart just moved in when you visit.

1.89 mi. Right on SE Ladd.

2.23 mi. Right into the center roundabout. The best part about getting lost in Ladd's Addition's diamond-patterned streets is stumbling across one of its four official Portland Rose Test Gardens. As you ride around the center roundabout, you can see each garden a few blocks away along SE 16th and SE Harrison. Explore if you wish before continuing on, but don't get too lost before returning here. Turn right to continue on SE Ladd (halfway around the center roundabout from where you entered).

2.61 mi. Left on SE Division and right on SE 21st. (The crosswalk is helpful at this busy and complicated intersection.)

2.74 mi. Left on SE Clinton ❷—a neighborhood greenway loaded with great shops and restaurants.

3.51 mi. Left on SE 34th.

3.9 mi. Cross SE Division. If the name "Hawthorne" isn't on everyone's tongue as much as it used to be, it's only because other places have asserted themselves in the pantheon of must-see Portland neighborhoods. SE Division is as red hot as they come. The only drawback, as is true of most of Portland's higher traffic and narrow shopping streets, is that riding a bike on Division is a *very* dangerous idea. Continue on 34th.

4.1 mi. Cross SE Hawthorne. Like Alberta in Northeast Portland, Hawthorne Street has so much cachet that any address within a mile is referred to as "Hawthorne." Hawthorne led the inner-city revitalization movement, first attracting young people interested in living in a place where they could get around exclusively by bike. Soon fun and eclectic businesses followed, filling the solid and historic streetcar-era storefronts between SE 30th and SE César Chavez. Today, businesses line nearly the entire length of the street from the foot of Mt. Tabor to the Willamette River. Continue on SE 34th.

4.41 mi. Cross SE Belmont. "The first trolley line on Portland's east side in 1888 and the first bike corrals in 2008" is how the local business association describes Hawthorne's lesser-known and compact twin. One standout is the funky Avalon Theatre (3451 SE Belmont) with its nickel arcade and second-run movie screens. Don't attempt to bike on Belmont; park your ride and explore from there.

❷

Clinton Street is a bike rider's paradise. While still relatively low-key, it has lots of great restaurants, cafes, and shops, in addition to being bike and pedestrian friendly. The action centers around SE 26th where you'll find the 1915 Clinton Street Theater showing art films and popular classics. The Rocky Horror Picture Show has played weekly since 1978 with theater-approved props including rice, a wedding ring, flashlights, rubber gloves, noisemakers, toilet paper, toast (dry, not buttered), playing cards, and a bell. The Clinton is also home to the annual Filmed By Bike festival featuring bike-themed short films from around the world. Every April hundreds of bikes converge on the Clinton for the festival's opening night party.

4.59 mi. Left on SE Washington and right on SE 33rd.

4.9 mi. Across from SE Pine, turn right into Laurelhurst Park. In 2001 Laurelhurst became the first city park to ever be placed on the National Register of Historic Places. For many years, Firwood Lake in the middle of the park hosted the coronation of the Rose Festival Queen on boats and decorated rafts.

5.26 mi. Exit the park diagonally across from where you entered and cross SE César Chavez on SE Ankeny.

5.42 mi. Left on SE 41st. As you cross NE Glisan, to your left is Coe Circle. The Joan of Arc Statue in the center of the circle—donated in 1925 by Portland doctor and philanthropist Henry Waldo Coe—is a memorial to the Americans who died in France during World War I (it's made from the original mold used for the statue in Paris). The circle is not easy to access, rendering this a "look out of the corner of your eye so as not to wreck" kind of a park.

5.88 mi. Left on NE Royal.

6.3 mi. Right on NE Flanders.

6.61 mi. Left on NE 32nd.

6.87 mi. Right on SE Ankeny. A few blocks later, cross NE 28th, another vibrant and revitalizing shopping street anchored by the 1923 Art Deco Laurelhurst Theater a block to your right. Best to explore busy NE 28th on foot before continuing on Ankeny.

7.54 mi. At SE 20th is Citybikes. This venerable worker-owned bike shop has been around since 1986—a time when riding a bike in Portland was an act of protest. Its sister shop, Citybikes Annex, is down the hill. At any point, you can cut one block to the right to busy E Burnside ❸. It's not a very safe biking street, but interesting shops and restaurants abound.

7.96 mi. Cross busy SE 12th, 11th, and Sandy.

8.26 mi. Right on SE 6th.

8.34 mi. Left on NE Couch, which becomes the bike lane across the Burnside Bridge. As you cross Grand, a large LED sign by the stop light proclaims "Turning vehicle yield to bike." Riding across, you get the full frontal view of the Portland, Oregon sign. If the holidays are near, by night the stag's nose will be blinking red for you.

9.01 mi. Right on NW 2nd and right on NW Couch.

9.1 mi. Turn right on NW 1st, dismount and walk under the Burnside Bridge.

9.15 mi. Back to the start.

Believe it or not, East Burnside used to be pretty much empty except for a strip club, antiques emporium, and the smell of downtown worker's car exhaust as they fled for the suburbs. Things have changed: Brewery? Pizza? Hot bar, cafe, vintage clothing store, sushi? Restaurant of the year? Community-powered radio station? Hip motel, diner, bar, and basement music venue—all in one? Skeleton key for a 1909 Craftsman? Russian-owned bar with naked women and expensive drinks? Done.

THE TWO BUTTES: KELLY AND POWELL

STEELE ST
SE RAMONA ST

11.02
miles

DISTANCE

EASY
194 feet

DIFFICULTY & ELEVATION GAIN

SCAVENGER HUNT

STARTING POINT

Lents/SE Foster Rd
MAX Station (east of
92nd Ave between
Foster Road and
Ramona Street)

A red basketball
court made from
ground-up shoe
soles

....

A little monkey
puzzle tree ("it
would puzzle
a monkey to
climb it")

....

A bike hanging over
a garage door

....

TRANSIT AND PARKING

TriMet's MAX Green Line stop at the Lents/SE Foster Rd station.
TriMet buses 10, 14, and 71 stop on SE Powell just below the
MAX station. Street parking is easy to find throughout the
neighborhood.

THIS TOUR TAKES ADVANTAGE of blissfully car-free
paths and quiet suburban streets to explore an area
of East Portland visually dominated by two green-covered
buttes—Kelly and Powell—both part of the Boring Lava
Field, an extinct volcanic area with as many as fifty lava
vents including Mt. Tabor, Rocky Butte, and Mt. Scott. For-
tunately (or not), the lava domes sound more dangerous
and fiery than they are in reality. No lava, dinosaurs, or circling Pterodactyls on this ride, just green trees and 1970s
ranch homes. The closest we'll get to wild on this tour may
be the little sheep farm nestled against the swell of Powell
Butte, the herd bleating among the farm buildings, grazing,
and fertilizing as they go.

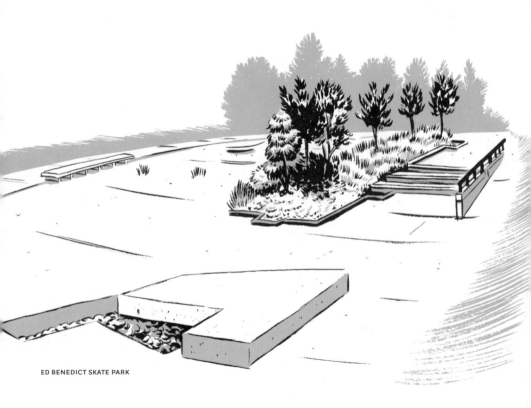

ED BENEDICT SKATE PARK

The ride starts in the Lents Town Center, the struggling heart of the pioneer-era city of Lents, today fighting to recover its former glory. Lents was settled in the 1880s by farmers attracted to the flat arable land, water supplies, and proximity to Portland markets. The arrival of the train along today's Springwater Corridor created better access to the area and spurred development. But after growing to 10,000 inhabitants, it was annexed by Portland in 1912, then promptly forgotten and neglected for decades. Lying in the midst of a transportation jumble (Interstate 205, Powell Boulevard, Foster Road, 82nd Avenue, the I-205 path, MAX, and the Springwater Corridor) Lents is the perfect place for an urban center. The Lents/SE Foster Rd MAX stop is one of the few on the Green Line with very little parking because it is envisioned as a transit point primarily for pedestrians rather than commuters leaving their cars. The stop is part of the city's Lents Town Center Urban Renewal Area, which funds a variety of projects aimed at attracting businesses and residents. The city's website calls the Lents of the future "a vibrant, mixed-use, pedestrian-scaled neighborhood that is a walkable and business friendly place to live, work and shop." Buy your new house or business building now while supplies last!

0.0 mi. Start on the Lents/SE Foster Rd MAX station platform. Looking over the rail at the cluster of buildings below is the town of Lents ❶, founded in 1892. With your back to the train, turn right on the I-205 Multi-Use Path, which runs for more than 16 miles from Vancouver, Washington, to Clackamas Town Center.

0.33 mi. Turn right and loop around to get on the pedestrian bridge and cross I-205. Continue heading east on SE Steele.

0.69 mi. Left on SE 100th. Bloomington Park on your right has restrooms and water fountains.

1.08 mi. Cross SE Holgate. Ahead of you is the Kelly Butte Natural Area, which looks much as it would have when pioneer—and namesake—Clinton Kelly settled here in 1848. "Natural Area" in Portland Parks and Recreation speak means the park isn't developed, at least not anymore. Kelly Butte's secret is far darker than mere development. A sealed up concrete bunker on its summit once held a civil defense emergency operations center used during the early days of the Cold War, and which was featured in the foreboding nuclear war doomsday film "A Day Called X." Intrepid urban adventurers sometimes venture behind its gates to hike the lonely road to its sealed entrance, bringing back stories of spooky forest and eerie quiet.

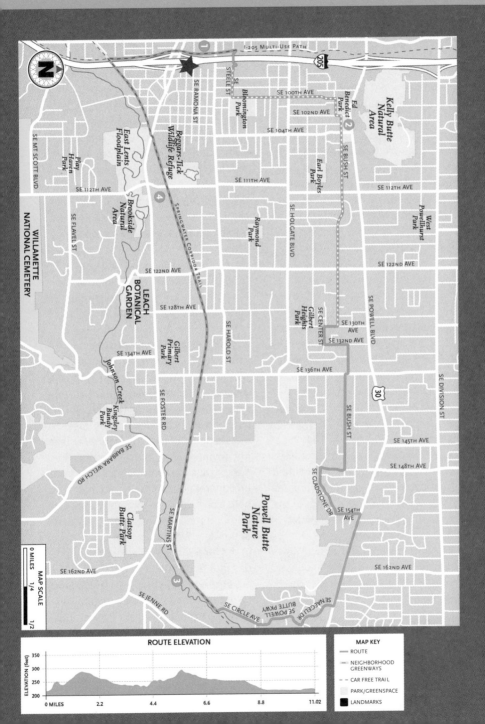

SE MT SCOTT BLVD

WILLAMETTE NATIONAL CEMETERY

I-205 MULTI-USE PATH

Kelly Butte Natural Area

SE RAMONA ST

SE STEELE ST

SE 100TH AVE

SE 102ND AVE

SE 104TH AVE

Bloomington Park

Ed Benedict Park

SE BENEDICT ST

East Lents Floodplain

Play Haven Park

Beggars-Tick Wildlife Refuge

SE 111TH AVE

Earl Boyles Park

West Powellhurst Park

SE 112TH AVE

SE 112TH AVE

Brookside Natural Area

SPRINGWATER CORRIDOR TRAIL

Raymond Park

SE HOLGATE BLVD

SE 122ND AVE

SE 122ND AVE

SE FLAVEL ST

SE 122ND AVE

LEACH BOTANICAL GARDEN

SE 128TH AVE

Gilbert Heights Park

SE POWELL BLVD

Gilbert Primary Park

SE HAROLD ST

SE CENTER ST

SE 130TH AVE

SE 132ND AVE

SE 134TH AVE

SE 136TH AVE

Johnson Creek

Kingsley Bundy Park

SE FOSTER RD

SE BUSH ST

30

SE DIVISION ST

SE BARBARA WELCH RD

SE MARTINS ST

Powell Butte Nature Park

SE GLADSTONE DR

SE 145TH AVE

SE 148TH AVE

Clatsop Butte Park

SE 154TH AVE

SE 162ND AVE

SE JENNE RD

SE CIRCLE AVE

SE POWELL BUTTE PKWY

SE 162ND AVE

SE NAGEL/DR

MAP SCALE

0 MILES   1/4   1/2

N

ROUTE ELEVATION

ELEVATION (feet)

350
300
250
200

0 MILES   2.2   4.4   6.6   8.8   11.02

MAP KEY

ROUTE

NEIGHBORHOOD GREENWAYS

– – CAR FREE TRAIL

PARK/GREENSPACE

LANDMARKS

Why all the Ed Benedict love around here? One block north of the route, SE Powell lies on what was intended to become the Mt. Hood freeway, stretching from downtown Portland to Gresham. When the freeway was defeated in 1974, local politician Ed Benedict vowed to have a park built on land purchased by the city for the freeway. The skateboard park in Ed Benedict Park—constructed with recycled and sustainable materials and featuring native plant landscaping and on-site stormwater drainage planters—has been called "the first environmentally sensitive skate plaza ever constructed." The Portland Memory Garden (in the southeast corner of the park) is designed for and dedicated to people with Alzheimer's disease and other memory problems. Next door is the 50-plot Ed Benedict Community Garden.

1.41 mi. Right on SE Bush. This is the beginning of a sweet low-traffic bike route marked with frequent sharrows.

1.5 mi. Turn left on SE 102nd and right where the unmarked path picks up in Ed Benedict park on the other side of the street. Several parks and sites along this stretch south of Powell have the name Ed Benedict in common.

2.97 mi. Right on SE 130th.

3.07 mi. Left on SE Center and left on SE 132nd.

3.36 mi. Right on Bush. At SE 136th, jog right and then left to stay on Bush.

4.21 mi. Right on SE 148th.

4.38 mi. Left on SE Gladstone Dr. Here is a parking lot and entrance to the 600-acre Powell Butte Nature Park with its impressive wall of firs rising up behind the houses. In contrast with solitary Kelly Butte, Powell Butte is popular with hikers, bikers, equestrians, and cars too (a road leads to the summit).

4.73 mi. Left on SE 154th.

4.90 mi. Right on SE Powell. Busy Powell doubles as Highway 26, but it does have a wide bike lane. On your right you'll pass the road to the top of Powell Butte.

5.51 mi. Right on SE Naegeli.

5.80 mi. Right on SE Powell Butte, which dead ends at a green space.

6.15 mi. Cross the green space on the short unofficial trail to the street on the other side, SE Circle. Go right (straight away from the dirt trail) on Circle. This is serious horse territory and an excellent oasis of "country" biking in the city.

6.46 mi. Right onto the Springwater Corridor, a paved multi-use trail built on a former rail corridor, running alongside Johnson Creek. Shortly thereafter, pass Schweitzer Restoration Area ❸ on your left. This is the start of a long stretch of car-free riding. Enjoy it.

9.05 mi. Just before SE 111th is a 20-acre wetland, Beggars-tick Wildlife Refuge, named for one of its abundant residents. This plant (also called hairy beggar's tick or devil's beggar-tick) is known for its ability to hitch a ride on humans using its prickly spine. The refuge was once an illegal garbage dump—5000 cubic yards of boulders, gypsum board, concrete, and asphalt were removed in 1993—but the restored wetlands now serve as a refuge for migratory birds and as stormwater storage, once again preventing flooding. On the hillside across from the lush meadow and wetland, look for the red barn, greenhouses, and neatly planted rows of Zenger Farm ❹.

❸

As population density increased, Johnson Creek's seasonal floods damaged farms and homesteads more frequently, prompting the federal government to straighten its course and line its banks with stone, destroying fish and wildlife habitat in the process. In spite of these efforts, the creek continued to flood regularly. In 2009 the city restored the section between SE 158th and SE 138th, called the Schweitzer Restoration Area. The marshy grassland allows water to spread out that would otherwise flood someone's backyard, business, or a road. Trees planted on the banks shade the water, keeping temperature-sensitive fish cool and happy. As part of the process, Environmental Services staff inventoried the fish in the wetland and found nearly 1400. Don't ask me how they did it.

Zenger Farm was first owned in the nineteenth century by Jacob Johnson—a sawmill operator for whom Johnson Creek is named—as part of his 320-acre donation land claim. The land was purchased in 1913 by Ulrich Zenger, a Swiss dairy farmer. When he died in 1954, the farm went to his son, Ulrich Zenger Jr. who wanted to protect the land from commercial development and preserve it as a farm. The land was purchased by Portland in 1994 in order to preserve the farm and its wetland as a collection point for the area's stormwater. Today, Friends of Zenger Farm uses the 10-acre wetland and 6-acre organic farming operation to teach young people, farmers, and families about sustainable agriculture, wetland ecology, food security, healthy eating, and local economic development.

9.83 mi. Cross SE Foster using the crosswalk. A few yards to the left, a bridge over Johnson Creek affords great views of the East Lents Floodplain Restoration Project. Here, earth was excavated to allow for drainage, while coconut netting (to control erosion) was laid along the banks, and ash tree stakes jabbed into the ground (the stakes will take root and grow). Meanwhile, dozens of logs and stumps were placed haphazardly along the banks to provide hiding places for young Coho salmon and other fish.

10.45 mi. Just past the I-205 underpass, turn right on the I-205 Multi-Use Path.

11.02 mi. Back to the start.

RIDE

19 MT. TABOR'S SHADOW

ROAD NOTES Riding can be somewhat challenging because of the number of busy streets to cross: 82nd, Burnside, Division, Glisan, Stark, and Washington. The city has worked to make these crossings easier for bicyclists and pedestrians, but you'll see there's still work to be done.

THE NEIGHBORHOODS SURROUNDING Portland's iconic cinder cone, 636-foot-tall Mt. Tabor, are outside the buzz of more well-known neighborhoods mere blocks to the west, if only because redevelopment—"hip-development"—generally started in the city center and worked its way outward. As this ride makes an east-to-west clockwise circuit, you'll go from passing newer homes to older and back to newer again. There are plenty of reasons to leave time for a meal on this tour as acclaimed restaurants continue to repopulate Stark Street's historic business district, and Portland's "new" Chinatown on 82nd is where knowledgeable food lovers flock.

If you'd like to increase your exercise, the Mt. Tabor extension adds 3.34 miles and 436 feet of elevation. It's a climb, but the views from the top are a classic Portland experience and well worth the effort.

SCAVENGER HUNT

A shiny metal gate with Chinese characters

....

A statue of Benjamin Franklin

....

A weathervane of shiny golden geese

....

STARTING POINT
SE Main Street MAX Station (1119 SE 96th Avenue)

8.2
miles

DISTANCE
(11.54 miles with Mt. Tabor extension)

EASY
121 feet

DIFFICULTY & ELEVATION GAIN
(hard with Mt. Tabor extension. 557 feet)

TRANSIT AND PARKING

TriMet's MAX Green Line stops at the SE Main Street station. TriMet bus 15 stops on SE 96th across from the MAX station. Look for street parking just south of the start on SE Market, or park across from the MAX station at Mall 205 (just be sure to buy something at one of the many local stores).

HARVEY SCOTT ON TOP OF MT. TABOR

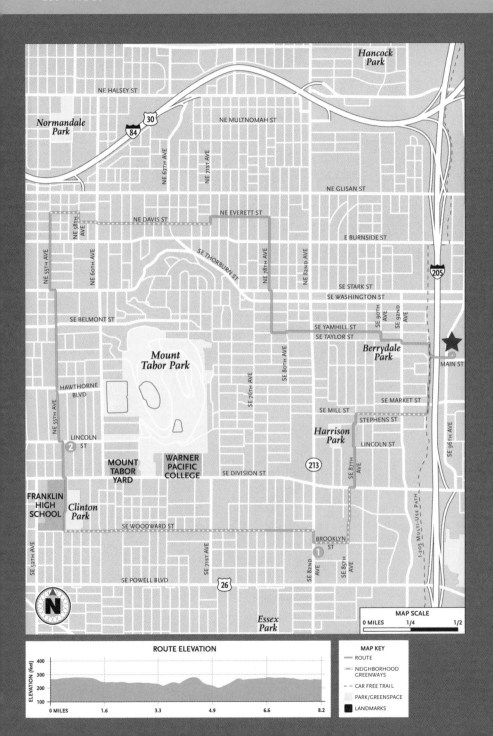

0.0 mi. Begin at the Main Street MAX station. Cross SE 96th, go up the corkscrew ramp, and ride across the bridge that goes over I-205.

0.29 mi. Turn left on the I-205 Multi-Use Path. Metro (the regional government), the Oregon Department of Transportation, and Friends of Trees, a local nonprofit, have teamed up to plant thousands of trees and install lighting to make the path greener, quieter, and safer. The tree-covered berm separating you from the freeway contributes to this much more pleasant biking experience.

0.61 mi. Right on SE Mill.

0.99 mi. Left on SE 87th. As 87th jogs right at SE Stephens, you'll pass Harrison Park and the Taborvilla Little League ball field.

1.4 mi. Cross SE Division using the pedestrian- and bike-only crossing signal light, handily located right next to you as you pull up to the crosswalk. Cross the street and turn right on the cycle track. Turn right then left on SE 85th.

You're now in the middle of Portland's eastern, unofficial "Chinatown," with plentiful Chinese, Korean, Vietnamese, Thai, Laotian, Filipino, and Japanese shops, restaurants, and businesses. The mini-mall half a block to the left at 8733 SE Division, for example, contains the offices of both Chinese and Thai community newspapers, a Chinese herbalist, a bubble tea shop, and an excellent (lunch only) dim sum restaurant—go in for a tummy-filling and mouthwatering experience you won't soon forget.

1.7 mi. Right on SE Brooklyn.

1.88 mi. At the intersection with ultra-busy SE 82nd ❶, turn right on the sidewalk (riding in the street would be suicide). One block ahead on the right is Fubonn, Portland's massive Asian market, well worth perusing. When you're done, cross SE 82nd onto SE Woodward.

2.1 mi. Here at SE 79th is one of Portland's inexplicably frequent unpaved roads. In this case it's only two out of the next three blocks.

3.32 mi. From Woodward, turn right into the parking lot for Franklin High School, across from SE 55th, and just past the tennis courts. Continue straight down the parking lot and along the path between the track and soccer fields. If the gate is open, turn left just before the track to see a statue of ole' Ben himself and his sweet view of the neighborhood and Mt. Tabor.

3.60 mi. Cross SE Division at 55th, or use the pedestrian light to the right across from SE 57th. Here, the trees immediately get bigger, the houses grander.

3.80 mi. At SE Lincoln, turn left then right to stay on 55th. This is the bike route extension to climb Mt. Tabor ❷.

4.08 mi. At the intersection of SE Hawthorne and 55th, look right to see the 1909 Western Seminary building. Behind the small balcony on the third floor is a ballroom, and the stained glass windows throughout the house are original. The commanding view down the entire length of Hawthorne must have given the original owner a real sense of power. This section of Hawthorne is the east end of a vibrant shopping district, up-and-coming since the early 1980s and still heading up, with eclectic shops, restaurants, cafes, and bars galore.

4.62 mi. At SE Stark, turn left and then right to stay on 55th.

❶

In a fit of wild optimism, the local business community has mounted street sign toppers proclaiming "82nd Avenue of Roses," a wistful reference to the 1920s when the street was lined with homes and their rose gardens, rather than used car lots and all the businesses that go along with them, strip malls, and motels. Not to mention, it's the center of the area's prostitution.

The bright side to the street is the thriving Asian community and its delicious restaurants and markets. At the numerous Vietnamese sandwich shops you can try a banh mi, a baguette typically filled with pork cold cuts, liver paste, cilantro, sliced chiles, julienned carrots, and pickled daikon radish. And a stroll through the aisles of Fubon is like a trip to another country. Besides the lumpy, prickly, and furry fruits and vegetables—and the bulgy-eyed fresh fish and animal feet, heads, and less-identifiable body parts in the meat case—you can peruse the giant cold drink case for a fresh coconut water, grass jelly drink, chrysanthemum tea, or exotic fruit juice (lychee, soursop, or guava).

② —————————

Here's the extension for Mt. Tabor:

1. From SE 55th, turn right on SE Lincoln.
2. Left on unmarked SE 64th (follow the "Mt. Tabor" bike sign).
3. Continue on the road as it turns sharply right.
4. Stay left on unmarked SE East Tabor (through the gates and uphill).
5. Stay left on unmarked SE North Tabor (uphill).
6. Sharp left on unmarked SE Tabor Summit and go around the locked gate.
7. Ride around SE Harvey Scott Circle. At the start of the circle is old Harvey himself in a statue by Gutzon Borglum, the man who sculpted Mt. Rushmore. It's all downhill from here.
8. Ride back down SE Tabor Summit.
9. Left at SE Mt. Tabor after the locked gate.
10. Left at unmarked SE Salmon Way.
11. Sharp right at SE Reservoir Loop.
12. Exit the park, SE Reservoir Loop becomes SE Salmon.
13. Rejoin the route at SE 55th.

5.05 mi. Right on NE Everett.

5.2 mi. Right on NE 58th and left on NE Davis. Cross busy NE 60th carefully.

5.98 mi. Left on NE 71st and right on NE Everett.

6.33 mi. Right on NE 78th. A few blocks later, cross E Burnside with care.

6.71 mi. Cross SE Stark and turn left (use the sidewalk since Stark is a one-way street) to stay on 78th. The Stark Business District, a classic Portland commercial center since its founding in 1889, is experiencing a steady comeback with shuttered stores coming back to life and new vibrant businesses popping up. This lively street is a delightful place to park the bike, stroll around, and have lunch and a beer (or coffee and a slice of pie) and soak up the small town atmosphere.

6.95 mi. Left on SE Yamhill.

7.53 mi. Right on SE 90th and left on SE Taylor.

7.71 mi. At SE 92nd, turn right and then left to stay on Taylor.

7.85 mi. Turn right on the I-205 Multi-Use Path and then turn left on the pedestrian trail to cross over the freeway.

8.2 mi. Back to the start.

RIDE

EAST PORTLAND AND WEST GRESHAM

ROAD NOTES In addition to the many nice protected crossings on this tour—complete with signs, zebra stripes, and button-activated lights—several unprotected busy street crossings still exist.

WHAT DO YOU GET WHEN you combine two fantastic car-free paths with the former farming neighborhoods of East Portland and West Gresham? An exploration of some lesser-known areas, including wildlife refuges, wetlands, and ancient lava domes. Beginning in the lively Wilkes East and Rockwood neighborhoods of West Gresham, you work your way along various livable streets and green parks, before jumping on the Gresham-Fairview Trail. After covering almost the entire length of this trail, you'll shift onto the Springwater Corridor, which follows the historic route of the rail line that ran from the foothills of Mt. Hood into Portland.

A 5-foot-tall gold-colored statue of Buddha

....

A rock painted like a turtle

....

A sculpture of a motorcycle

....

STARTING POINT
E 162nd Ave MAX Station (E Burnside Street and 162nd Avenue)

10.79
miles

DISTANCE

EASY
180 feet

DIFFICULTY & ELEVATION GAIN

LINNEMANN STATION

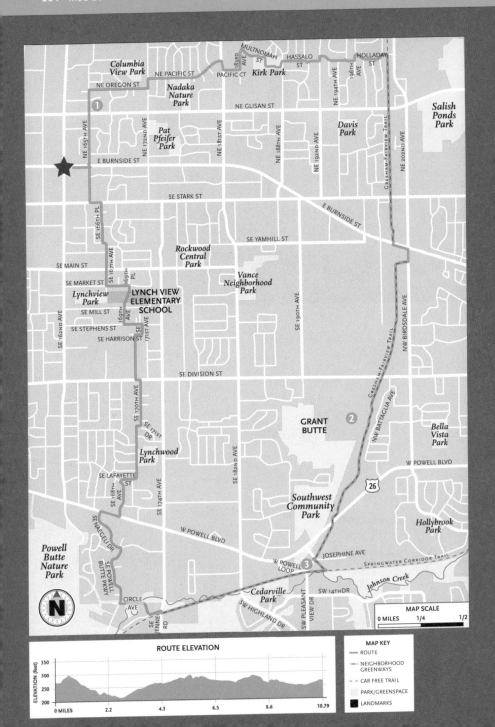

ROUTE ELEVATION

MAP SCALE
0 MILES   1/4   1/2

MAP KEY
— ROUTE
≈ NEIGHBORHOOD GREENWAYS
- - CAR FREE TRAIL
PARK/GREENSPACE
■ LANDMARKS

Kwan Yin Temple of Oregon serves Portland-area worshippers primarily from southeast Asia, including China, Taiwan, Laos, Vietnam, Cambodia, and Thailand. If you have time, make sure to go inside, the temple is full of statues of various Buddhist deities, demons, and mythical beings beneath a graceful curved beam ceiling. The monks welcome the curious every Sunday between 10 a.m. and noon, after which everyone sits down to a meal.

0.0 mi. Begin at the E 162nd Ave MAX station and ride east on Burnside. At NE 165th, cross Burnside on the track crossing and turn left on 165th.

0.47 mi. Cross NE Glisan. On the corner, behind the seated gold Buddha statue and the towering 20-foot-tall statue of Kwan Yin Bodhisattva, is a Buddhist temple of the same name.

0.61 mi. Right on NE Oregon.

0.96 mi. Left on NE 172nd, then turn right on NE Pacific St. A few blocks later, pass the green, peaceful, fir-scented 10-acre Nadaka Nature Park.

1.48 mi. Right on busy NE 181st and left (carefully) on NE Pacific Ct.

1.64 mi. Left on NE 183rd and right on NE Multnomah.

1.88 mi. Right into Kirk Park. Follow the path through the park (light on trees and heavy on lawn) and turn left at the Y intersection to exit the park on NE Hassalo (there's no curb cut).

2.25 mi. Stay on Hassalo by turning left and then right at NE 191st and NE 192nd.

2.55 mi. Left on NE 196th and right on NE Holladay.

2.8 mi. Right onto the Gresham-Fairview Trail. As of 2013, this fantastic 3.3-mile-long trail extends from the Springwater Corridor to NE Halsey, but it will eventually connect with the 40-Mile Loop on Marine Drive.

In the next mile on the trail you'll cross NE Glisan and SE Stark (both unsigned) with nice crosswalk signals.

3.86 mi. Left on E Burnside for the short detour around TriMet's Ruby Junction maintenance yard (home base for MAX trains).

3.97 mi. Turn right on SE 202nd/NW Birdsdale and then sharply right back onto the Gresham-Fairview Trail, just over the MAX tracks. For a few minutes the trail is wedged between high chain link fences, but the industrial zone quickly gives way to an area of wetland restoration.

4.78 mi. Cross NW Division and continue on the trail. On your right is Grant Butte , one of the area's many Boring Lava domes, created between 100,000 and 6 million years ago. The townhomes on the left take full advantage of the killer views.

5.6 mi. At busy W Powell, stay right at the Y intersection to cross over Powell on the solid and attractive bridge. Bridges for bikes and pedestrians to cross busy streets like this are a testament to how many people created the political will to find the money to get the bridge built. You can see at least six of the area's Boring Lava domes from the bridge.

5.94 mi. Left at the sign marked "Springwater Corridor" and go through the gate. The horses in the 66-acre pasture to the left belong to the nonprofit Mounted Explorer Post 686. This group offers high school students the opportunity to learn about all aspects of horse ownership, from dentistry, shoeing, and grooming, to, of course, riding.

6.0 mi. Right on the paved multi-use Springwater Corridor Trail. In a few hundred yards on your right is Linnemann Station ❸.

At the base of Grant Butte is the lush, natural, and wildlife-rich Fairview Creek Headwaters. Fairview Creek runs to the north and eventually empties into Fairview Lake near the Columbia River. This entire area was once part of a system of wetlands feeding into the Columbia, called the Columbia Slough Watershed. Over the last 150 years these wetlands have been drained for housing and businesses. Renewed interest in water and air quality, saving species of animals that are disappearing due to loss of habitat, recreation opportunities, and scenery are all causing area residents to ask local governments to restore and protect these areas. This watershed is the endangered western painted turtle's last remaining habitat east of the Willamette River.

3

Linnemann station is the last remaining actual trolley station on the Springwater Corridor, named for two German immigrants, Catharine and her husband, John. They started out on the Oregon Trail in 1852, finally arriving in Portland on foot, pulling their wagon by hand after their two oxen and fellow traveler died during the journey. The couple took out a 320-acre donation land claim, and John walked the 17 miles from his tailor shop in downtown Portland every weekend to join Catharine in their log cabin near here. Catharine spent her time clearing the land, planting the garden, and eventually becoming Gresham's first woman postmaster and first librarian. Today, Linnemann Station is used as a community center and is a great starting point for walks, jogs, and rides on the path.

7.04 mi. Right at SE Jenne and immediately left on SE Circle. Circle feels like a magical street in the middle of the country, with horses grazing in roadside pastures, an idyllic bridge over wild Johnson Creek, and a big green barn.

7.35 mi. Turn sharply right across the narrow grass strip onto unmarked SE Powell Butte.

7.7 mi. Left on SE Naegeli.

7.97 mi. Right on SE Powell (it's busy but the shoulder is wide) and left on SE 168th. If you're uncomfortable crossing Powell here, continue to SE 174th, which has a traffic light, cross and double back.

8.3 mi. Right on SE Lafayette, which turns left and becomes SE 170th. Pass darkly forested, cedar-pathed, peaceful Lynchwood Park.

8.73 mi. At SE 171st Dr, turn right and then left to stay on 170th.

8.99 mi. Left (carefully) on SE Division and right back onto 170th.

9.28 mi. Right on SE Harrison and left on SE 171st. Bike carefully on the block of gravel here (think of it as a free roller coaster in summer or mud puddle adventure in not-summer).

9.38 mi. Left on SE Stephens then right on SE 169th.

9.6 mi. At SE Mill go straight on the path through Lynch View Elementary School's parking lot, which welcomes you in Russian, Spanish, and English. Exit on SE 169th.

9.73 mi. Left on SE Market.

9.88 mi. Right on unmarked SE 167th.

10.1 mi. Right on SE 166th Pl.

10.35 mi. Left on SE Stark and right on SE 165th.

10.62 mi. Cross the MAX tracks and turn left on SE Burnside.

10.79 mi. Back to the start.

21 WOODSTOCK, LENTS, AND THE FOSTER TRIANGLE

10.1
miles

DISTANCE

EASY
125 feet

DIFFICULTY & ELEVATION GAIN

STARTING POINT
SE Holgate Blvd
MAX Station (9369
SE Holgate Boule-
vard)

Walls of colorful
tiles of plants and
animals

....

A round tower
with a rooster
weathervane

....

A pig weathervane

....

TRANSIT AND PARKING

TriMet's MAX Green Line stops at the SE Holgate station. TriMet
bus 17 stops on SE Holgate next to the MAX station. Look for
street parking on SE 92nd by Lents Park.

PERHAPS NO OTHER AREA of Portland has been targeted as having the building blocks for a successful neighborhood center as much as the areas you visit on the eastern half of this ride. Originally its own city, Lents was eventually annexed by Portland, but its infrastructure and economic opportunity remained neglected. Today however, memories of "felony flats" are fading fast as the city invests millions to make Lents an attractive live-work neighborhood and model community. By the same token, Woodstock and other neighborhoods in the western half are already there, with comfortable cute Craftsman homes, green parks, and small quirky shops.

This ride also takes advantage of the I-205 Multi-Use Path and the Springwater Corridor Trail. Each are different in character but both make for smooth, safe riding.

CARTLANDIA!

The Springwater Corridor is a paved multi-use trail built on a former rail corridor. By 1910 the original rail line had 161 miles of rail and carried 16,000 passengers each year hauling people and farm produce to Portland markets, and connecting the many communities and towns that developed along and because of it. Passenger service was discontinued in 1958 and much of the Springwater Corridor was acquired in 1990. Construction of the 21-mile trail was completed in 2000, making it the preeminent biking and walking path in the metro area. Nowhere else around can you feel like you're taking a spin in the country while traversing a two-million plus person metropolis.

0.0 mi. Begin at the SE Holgate Blvd MAX platform and ride through the TriMet parking lot to SE Holgate. The giant metal sculpture of stainless steel lanterns looming between the tracks and parking lot represent safety and security in the dark, and symbolize the richness of positive social interaction that a neighborhood brings.

0.15 mi. Cross SE Holgate and ride straight along the I-205 Multi-Use Path (keep the freeway on your left). The path runs parallel to TriMet's MAX Green Line and Interstate 205, making it a truly multi-modal transportation corridor.

0.55 mi. Right on unmarked SE Steele (notice the pedestrian bridge on the left). Pass by Lents Park, occupying more than 38 acres on the site of a former gravel quarry.

0.8 mi. Left on SE 88th.

0.98 mi. Right on SE Ellis and left on SE 87th. As you approach busy SE Foster notice the proliferation of sharrows: the city is taking safety and usability seriously here. Use the pedestrian crossing light (the button is handily within reach for bicyclists) to help you across Foster. The heart of the Lents Town Center project, designed to bring new life to the entire area is located a few blocks away at 92nd and Foster.

1.47 mi. At SE Duke, turn right and then left to stay on 87th. Expansive Glenwood Park on the left has bathrooms and water fountains next to its big ball fields.

1.98 mi. Left on SE Flavel and right onto the Springwater Corridor Trail ❶. Unlike the I-205 path, the Springwater runs through and between neighborhoods. In many places it is fully lined with lush trees and brush, with rabbit trails leading to homeless camps that have been the source of some scary reports by late night cyclists.

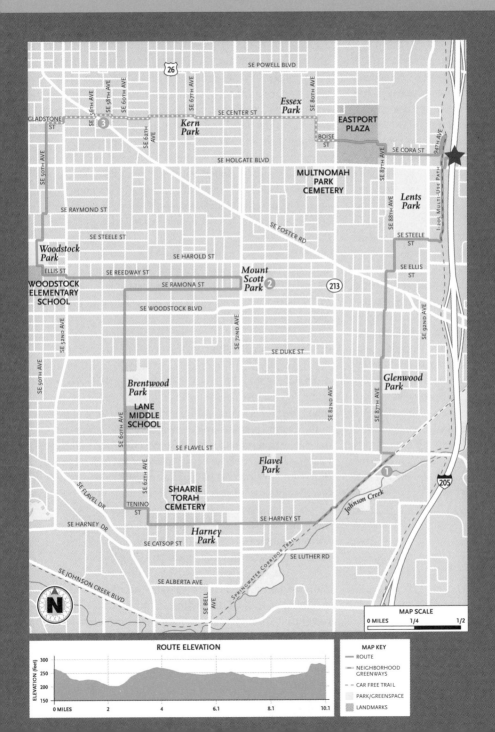

2.49 mi. After crossing SE 82nd, Cartlandia—a food cart pod in a former used car lot—is on your left. This bustling pod has up to two dozen carts serving delicious food from all over the world, along with covered seating, a beer garden complete with a trailer with a big screen TV for the games, and an ATM to pay for it all. Cartlandia even welcomes horses (from the Springwater Corridor apparently).

2.62 mi. Exit the Springwater Corridor by turning right on SE Harney (the street sign is on a wooden post on the bike path). Harney has a similar country-like vibe as the corridor, partly because of the lack of sidewalks, partly because of the relaxed attitude of some of the houses. Home auto repair is a big hobby throughout this area.

3.04 mi. Cross SE 72nd. If you want to relive your rural childhood with a pop and a bag of Funyuns, a few blocks to the left at SE Clatsop is a market that feels like a country store. Soon you'll pass Harney Park with big meadows and softball fields.

3.55 mi. Right on SE 62nd and left on SE Tenino. The towering trees at 6035 are perfectly placed on either side of the driveway, so the owner decided to use them as gate posts and hung their address number on one of them.

3.76 mi. Right on SE 60th. Several blocks later, just after Lane Middle School, you pass the Learning Gardens Laboratory. This PSU program offers kids and parents the opportunity to grow their own food and give excess from the harvest—hundreds of pounds a year—to those in need.

4.79 mi. Cross SE Woodstock carefully. (The fun, eclectic center of the Woodstock neighborhood is several blocks to the left.)

4.91mi. Right on SE Ramona.

5.39 mi. Left on SE 72nd. Here you run right into Mt Scott Park and Community Center, which, along with the neighborhood itself and the mountain/cinder cone on the horizon, is named for Harvey Scott ❷, the influential editor of the *Oregonian*. The community center has a great indoor swimming pool, complete with a lazy river that keeps kids squealing with delight all winter long. If you detour one block to

SE Harold, you'll find a bunch of vibrant businesses worth exploring, including a bike shop, a coffee shop and bakery, a venerable motorbike bar, and a Filipino market.

5.62 mi. Left on SE Reedway.

6.57 mi. Right on SE 52nd and left on SE Ellis.

6.73 mi. Right on SE 50th. The classically styled Woodstock Elementary has a Mandarin Chinese immersion program.

6.75 mi. Left on the path between the school and the edge of Woodstock Park. Then turn right at the path lined with huge Douglas fir trees and ride through the park.

6.93 mi. Exit the park by turning right on SE Steele, then left on 50th.

7.1 mi. Ignore the dead-end sign on 50th at SE Raymond and ride or walk your bike along the short gravel section.

7.37 mi. Still on 50th, cross SE Holgate carefully. If you're uncomfortable crossing here, turn right and right to 52nd, cross at the light and double back.

7.6 mi. Right on SE Gladstone. After one block, turn left on 52nd and right on SE Center.

2

Besides emigrating from Illinois in 1852, then walking to Forest Grove from Olympia to be the first person to graduate from Pacific University, Harvey Scott was editor of *The Oregonian* newspaper from 1865 to 1910. Harvey's opinion was so powerful that in an era when local politics were dominated by corruption and the newspaper was hardly more than pure editorial, he could almost be considered a separate branch of local government. Even after his death, his influence was not forgotten. The unveiling of the Harvey Scott statue on top of Mt. Tabor, 23 years after he died, was attended by 3000 people.

Even more influential over the long term was Harvey's older sister, Abigail Scott Duniway. Abigail and Harvey's parents were Oregon Trail pioneers in 1852, settling in the Willamette Valley town of Lafayette. Abigail married a farmer and had six children before her husband ended up crippled after a horse-team accident and Abigail had to support the family. She opened a boarding school, taught in a private school, and finally opened a millinery (hat) and "notions" shop before becoming so irate at the stories she encountered of the treatment of women in 1871 pioneer society that she moved to Portland to start a newspaper that fought for women's rights. She wrote, marched, and protested for 41 years, and in 1912, Oregon became the seventh state in the country to pass women's suffrage. This was eight years before the national law, thanks in large part to this strong-willed, brave, and tireless woman.

3

Foster, along with Powell and 82nd, has had many problems with pedestrians being hit by cars so the city is working hard to install more pedestrian- and bike-friendly crossings on these busy streets. The Foster Triangle, formed by SE Foster, SE Powell to the north, and SE 82nd to the east, is lined with businesses along these three streets, and garden-rich homes filling the middle. The neighborhood's eclectic and all-American feel is evidenced by the establishments populating the area where you cross Foster: a gun shop, a plumbing showroom, a dive bar called Smokey's Tavern, a music/art/dance space called the Day Theater, a taxidermy shop, and a hipster bar called Slingshot Lounge. Quite a mix.

7.90 mi. Cross SE Foster **3** at SE 56th using the crossing signal and the excellent (bright green) Copenhagen-left bike box. After crossing Foster, turn right to stay on Center. As the street zigzags, turn as needed to stay on Center. You'll pass Kern Park (no facilities) on the right and then Essex Park (bathroom and water fountain), home of the Sunrise Little League, on the left.

9.24 mi. Right on SE 80th and left on SE Boise. As you approach 82nd, you might get a "we're not in bikelandia anymore" feeling because of the tire and brake shops flanking you and the roaring river of cars.

9.34 mi. Cross SE 82nd (thank goodness for the bike-shaped pavement marking that senses metal and triggers the light). Boise leads you into Eastport Plaza with one of the only Wal-Marts in Portland, along with a large movie theater and dozens of other shops.

9.57 mi. Stay on Boise all the way to the back fence. Turn right, then left on the path next to Wal-Mart's back lot until you come out on unmarked SE 87th.

9.67 mi. After just a half block on 87th, turn left at the nearly hidden sidewalk before the big hill and come out on SE Cora. This sneaky end-around is the kind of thing I love. It looks like it's going to be a dead end just before it turns out to be an awesome way through a bad situation.

9.96 mi. From Cora, turn left on SE 94th. Turn right on the I-205 Multi-Use Path across from SE Boise.

10.05 mi. Make a U-turn left at SE Holgate and into the MAX parking lot.

10.1 mi. Back to the start.

22

RHODIES AND REEDIES TO SELLWOOD

STARTING POINT

SE 17th Avenue and
SE Mall Street

10.46 miles

DISTANCE

EASY 200 feet

**DIFFICULTY &
ELEVATION GAIN**

SCAVENGER HUNT

A lake in the middle
of a college campus

....

A Ferris wheel

....

TRANSIT AND PARKING

TriMet bus 17 stops on SE Holgate, and bus 70 stops on SE
17th—both are close to the start. The SE 17th and Holgate
station of the MAX Orange Line is scheduled to open in fall 2015.
Look for street parking near the station on side streets (SE Mall
and SE 16th).

ROAD NOTES Near the end of the route, SE 17th between
McLoughlin and Holgate is fairly busy with no bike lane so walking
or slowly riding on the sidewalk is a good choice here.

SET UP ON THE CLIFF above the shipyards, docks, and industry, the neighborhoods of inner southeast Portland became chopped up, cut off, and crisscrossed with transportation corridors early in the city's industrial boom. But unusual for the time, landowners and city planners reserved enough open space with natural waterways, hills, and gullies intact, landscaping them to create some of the most loved parks in the city. In the middle of it all sits a highly respected college that seeks to teach young people to learn and think for themselves.

Consider timing your ride with a nod to the Crystal Springs Rhododendron Garden. The Rhodies bloom from early March through the middle of June, with their peak over Mother's Day weekend, a nice coincidence for Oregon moms and their families. Take that as a hint!

THE BLUE BRIDGE ON THE
CAMPUS OF REED COLLEGE

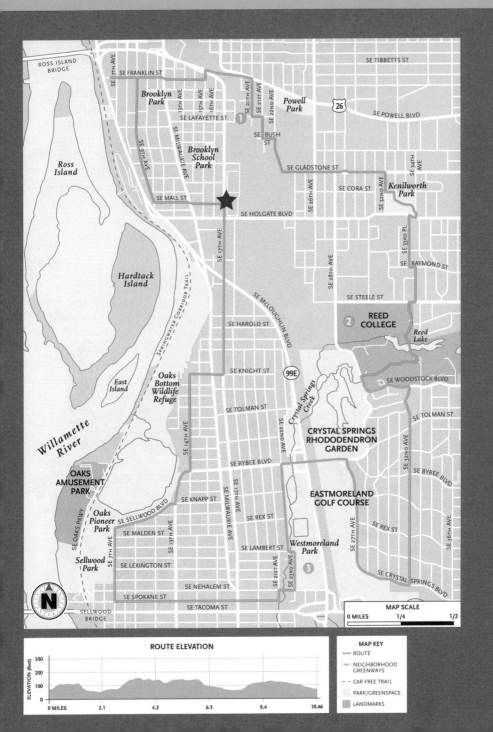

ROSS ISLAND
BRIDGE

SE FRANKLIN ST

SE 7TH AVE

*Brooklyn
Park*

SE 13TH AVE
SE 15TH AVE
SE 16TH AVE

SE LAFAYETTE ST

SE 20TH AVE
SE 21ST AVE
SE 22ND AVE

*Powell
Park*

SE TIBBETTS ST

US 26

SE POWELL BLVD

①

SE BUSH
ST

*Brooklyn
School
Park*

SE 9TH AVE

SE MILWAUKIE AVE

SE GLADSTONE ST

SE 24TH
AVE

*Ross
Island*

SE MALL ST

★

SE HOLGATE BLVD

SE 26TH AVE

SE CORA ST

SE 32ND AVE

*Kenilworth
Park*

SE 33RD PL

SPRINGWATER CORRIDOR TRAIL

*Hardtack
Island*

SE 17TH AVE

SE MCLOUGHLIN BLVD

SE 28TH AVE

SE RAYMOND ST

SE STEELE ST

② **REED
COLLEGE**

*Reed
Lake*

SE HAROLD ST

*East
Island*

*Oaks
Bottom
Wildlife
Refuge*

SE 14TH AVE

SE KNIGHT ST

99E

Crystal Springs Creek

SE WOODSTOCK BLVD

SE TOLMAN ST

*Willamette
River*

SE TOLMAN ST

SE 22ND AVE

**CRYSTAL SPRINGS
RHODODENDRON
GARDEN**

SE 32ND AVE

**OAKS
AMUSEMENT
PARK**

SE BYBEE BLVD

SE BYBEE BLVD

SE 36TH AVE

SE OAKS PKWY

*Oaks
Pioneer
Park*

SE SELLWOOD BLVD

SE KNAPP ST

SE 17TH AVE

SE MILWAUKIE AVE

SE REX ST

**EASTMORELAND
GOLF COURSE**

SE 27TH AVE

SE REX ST

SE 13TH AVE

SE MALDEN ST

SE 7TH AVE

SE LEXINGTON ST

SE LAMBERT ST

SE 21ST AVE

SE 23RD AVE

*Westmoreland
Park*

③

*Sellwood
Park*

SE NEHALEM ST

SE SPOKANE ST

SE TACOMA ST

SE CRYSTAL SPRINGS BLVD

SELLWOOD
BRIDGE

N

MAP SCALE

0 MILES   1/4   1/2

ROUTE ELEVATION

ELEVATION (feet)

300
200
100
0

0 MILES   2.1   4.2   6.3   8.4   10.46

MAP KEY

— ROUTE

NEIGHBORHOOD
GREENWAYS

– – CAR FREE TRAIL

PARK/GREENSPACE

LANDMARKS

0.0 mi. Begin at the corner of SE Mall and SE 17th in the Brooklyn neighborhood, founded in 1851 by pioneer Gideon Tibbets who named it "Brookland" for the many creeks, lakes, and the river running through his property. Over the decades the neighborhood has been gradually hemmed in on all sides by busy roads and railroads until it has become an island of sorts. Ride west on Mall (uphill).

0.14 mi. At SE Milwaukie, turn right and then left to stay on Mall.

0.32 mi. Right on SE 9th. The roar of cars tells you SE McLoughlin (Highway 99E) is just on the other side of the hedge. From here, Mcloughlin moves away from 9th and the traffic noise drops steadily away.

0.91 mi. Left on SE Franklin. Ride to the intersection with McLoughlin for a great view: downtown Portland to the right, Ross Island and the Ross Island Bridge ahead, as well as the South Waterfront neighborhood directly across and OHSU on the hillside.

1.07 mi. Return the way you came on SE Franklin. The 1890 farmhouse on the corner of 9th has an inviting porch shaded by big trees; it's easy to imagine cows placidly munching grass in the long-gone pasture.

1.36 mi. At Milwaukie, turn right and then left to stay on Franklin. Nearby is the iconic Aladdin Theater (3017 SE Milwaukie) a live-music venue that started out in 1928 as a vaudeville theater. Edelweiss Deli (on SE Powell and SE 12th) is a neighborhood gem and reminder that many of Brooklyn's early immigrants were German (several streets with German names were renamed during World War I). Stop in for a brat or just to admire the meat and cheese case, and perhaps yodel an order to the fräulein behind the counter.

1.57 mi. Left on SE 15th. Ride half a block and turn right on SE Powell, then ride under the railroad bridge on the wide but loud car-free path.

1.85 mi. Right on SE 20th. On the right, at the corner of SE 20th and Lafayette is your first opportunity to really see the elephant in Brooklyn's living room—the Brooklyn Intermodal Rail Yard ❶. Get off your bike and climb the stairs of the pedestrian overpass for a birds-eye view of the yards.

2.02 mi. Left on SE Lafayette and right on SE 21st.

2.17 mi. Left on SE Bush. On the corner of 21st and Bush is a house with a fun and funky homemade stucco garden shed and bike frame fence.

2.38 mi. Right on SE 22nd. The name changes to SE Gladstone as it curves left. The giant building is the headquarters for Fred Meyer, a Portland institution since 1922 when Frederick Grubmeyer—called "the last of the great American entrepreneurs" by the Wall Street Journal started selling coffee from a horse-drawn cart at farms and lumber camps. Freddie's now has more than 30,000 employees in 131 stores.

2.88 mi. Right on SE 32nd and left on SE Cora into Kenilworth Park. This park is named for *Kenilworth*, a novel by Sir Walter Scott, as are the Waverly and Woodstock neighborhoods and Ivanhoe Street. Ride diagonally through the park to 34th and Holgate.

3.19 mi. Exit the park by turning right on SE Holgate. Then take your first left on SE 33rd Pl.

3.44 mi. At Raymond, turn left and then right to stay on 33rd.

3.64 mi. Right on SE Steele and left on the road with the sign that says "Reed College ❷ North Parking Lot."

3.8 mi. The road dead ends at the second parking lot. Turn left on the bike path (left of the campus map at Bragdon Hall) and stay left until you come to the Blue Bridge over Reed Canyon, the wooded wetland in the center of campus. At one of the annual end-of-year parties, Reed students replaced the commonplace white bulbs with blue lights. The look was so captivating that the lights were never changed back.

Wonder why the Brooklyn Intermodal Rail Yard is here and not elsewhere? In 1956, the surrounding, more affluent neighborhoods were concerned the loud noise of train cars and horns, and the diesel fumes, would ruin their quality of life, so they had an injunction placed on Union Pacific Railroad limiting how far south trains could be assembled and forbidding new lines to be built. Brooklyn, then a poverty-stricken neighborhood, was not included in the lawsuit. Today, many of Oregon's famous Christmas trees are shipped from this yard around the country.

❷

Reed College, founded in 1908, is as close to an Ivy League school as Oregon can claim. "Reedies" are encouraged to bike to class among the brick Tudor Gothic buildings and their class sizes are limited to ten students per teacher. Reed is also the only US school with a nuclear reactor run by undergrads. A young Reed dropout named Steve Jobs drew inspiration from the calligraphy classes he took here, calling it "the magic that enlivens science." Besides Reed's standing as one of the best liberal arts colleges in the country, the Princeton Review habitually ranks Reed number one in its annual list of best colleges for "Birkenstock-Wearing, Tree-Hugging, Clove-Smoking Vegetarians." They forgot to mention the college's policy not to involve itself in students' extracurricular "self-medications," as long as they don't harm or embarrass another student.

3.92 mi. After crossing the bridge, turn left. At the traffic circle turn right, and then right again to ride alongside the front lawn of Eliot Hall. (The magnificent limestone and brick building was built in 1912 as the Arts and Sciences building but I think it looks like an English boarding school.). Stay left at the Y intersection at Winch hall.

4.12 mi. Take a soft left in front of the Tudor-Gothic arch with the griffin crest (Kerr Hall). Pass MacNaughton and Foster dorms on your left.

4.29 mi. Cross SE 28th into the Crystal Springs Rhododendron Garden parking lot. Originally called Shakespeare Island because of the plays performed there by Reed College students, the garden was officially established in 1950 with the goal of having a display and test garden for rhododendrons, much like the International Rose Test Garden in Washington Park. This lush paradise now features more than 2500 plants and the surrounding lake attracts many species of birds. Admission is free during the off-bloom season from Labor Day through February. Turn right on 28th to continue.

4.39 mi. Left on SE Woodstock. Immediately on your right is Parker House, a 30-room Arts and Crafts home built in 1929 and now used by Reed for visiting guests.

4.58 mi. Right on SE 32nd. Here is the Eastmoreland neighborhood. Can you say gargantuan Craftsman houses? These stunning examples of architecture look as well manicured and stately as when they were built in the 1920s. The neighborhood is also full of cute English-style cottages tucked behind tree tunnels.

5.52 mi. Right on SE Crystal Springs. As you come down the hill, the second oldest golf course in Oregon is on your left. Opened in 1917, the Eastmoreland Golf Course greens sit on former dairy pastureland and are full of trees, streams, and lakes. The trees have all been trimmed up high from the ground, affording a long and lush view of green grass and tree trunks.

6.29 mi. Left on SE Bybee and cross over the railroad tracks, MAX Orange Line, and SE McLoughlin.

6.62 mi. Left on SE 22nd. Here you find the attraction-packed, 42-acre Westmoreland City Park .

7.03 mi. Left on unmarked SE Lambert, cross Crystal Springs Creek and turn right on SE 23rd.

7.24 mi. Right at the T intersection (on unmarked SE Nehalem) and left on SE 21st. As 21st turns right it becomes SE Spokane, where you can get a last glimpse of the creek (and perhaps a duckling sunning itself on a rock).

At SE 13th is one of the two main shopping districts of the Westmoreland-Sellwood neighborhood, Sellwood for short. Another early rival to Portland, Sellwood was its own town until it was absorbed by the city in 1893. Sellwood is a wonderfully livable neighborhood, characterized by the sheer density and quality of antique stores, small independent shops, and restaurants along charming streets.

8.19 mi. Right on SE 7th. A few blocks further is the Sellwood Pool and Park. The pool, open since 1910, originally admitted boys and girls separately on alternating days. The park next door was once home to a horse racing track.

Westmoreland City Park was once a wetland, like Eastmoreland next door, before being turned into a dairy, brickyard, and airstrip known as Broom Field. In 1936, the city built the casting pond, model yacht lagoon (known as the Duck Pond, the "yachts" are now radio-controlled boats), a fly caster's club house, bridges, and the athletic fields. Later they added the baseball stadium, lawn bowling, croquet and the gravel court, (used for the French style of bocce called *pétanque*.) The pond is fed by Crystal Springs Creek, and the birdlife mostly consists of the big and aggressive Canada Geese, and whatever ducks are tough enough to hang with the big birds.

8.53 mi. As SE 7th turns right and becomes SE Sellwood pause for great views of the churchlike glass spires of the convention center in the distance and the barnlike roller rink of Oaks Park. Below and to the left is the Oaks Bottom Wildlife Refuge, and to the far right is the vividly repainted mural on the side of Wilhelm's Portland Memorial Funeral Home.

8.85 mi. Left on busy SE 13th. As 13th turns right, the bustling intersection of SE Milwaukie and SE Bybee is another block ahead. This vibrant small-town hold-out has a wonderful mix of old and new: taverns, recognizable local chains, craft brewpubs, a hardware store, and the single screen 1926 Moreland Theatre. In the parking lot at 14th and Bybee, the Moreland Farmers Market is held every Wednesday, mid-May through September.

9.04 mi. Left on SE 14th, which turns right and becomes SE Knight.

9.64 mi. Left on SE 17th. Without a bike lane, 17th can be unpleasant, especially between SE McLoughlin and SE Holgate. The sidewalk is a good alternative to street biking here.

10.07 mi. Cross SE McLoughlin.

10.46 mi. Left on SE Mall and back to the start.

23 MILWAUKIE AND THE SPRINGWATER CORRIDOR

THE RIDE BEGINS IN the revitalizing downtown of historic Milwaukie. Enterprising pioneer and founder Lot Whitcomb was reportedly so taken with the city of Milwaukee, Wisconsin, that he bestowed (almost) the same name upon his new town in 1847. Today's downtown is anchored by Dark Horse Comics (publisher of Star Wars, Buffy, and Hellboy), which takes up three city blocks including a big comic book store complete with three dimensional superhero figurines.

From downtown, you'll explore the industrial area on the north side of town before jumping on Springwater Corridor and into the former-farmland neighborhoods. Among the mid-century ranch houses, you'll see classic homes that offer a glimpse back to the days when a few farmhouses sat in the middle of seemingly endless orchards or fields bursting with produce. The route drops back down across the busy main roads before exploring a particularly alluring section of the Willamette River.

Note: Few, if any, public bathrooms are available on this route. City Hall or a business on Main near the start are your best bets.

SCAVENGER HUNT

Mannequins of aliens in a window

An American flag–colored roof and bald eagle mural

A horse-drawn streetcar

STARTING POINT

Milwaukie City Hall
(10722 SE Main
Street, Milwaukie
97222)

10.08
miles

DISTANCE

MODERATE
223 feet

**DIFFICULTY &
ELEVATION GAIN**

**TRANSIT AND
PARKING**

TriMet buses 28, 29,
30, 31, 32, 70, and 75
all stop near City Hall.
As of 2015, TriMet's
MAX Orange Line will
serve the Milwaukie
Main Street station (SE
Main and SE Jack-
son). Look for street
parking on SE Main or
park in the lot across
from City Hall (except
on Sundays when the
market is open).

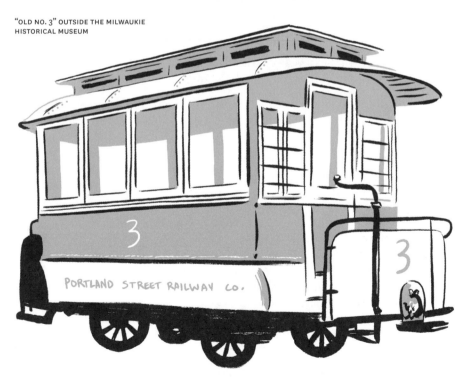

"OLD NO. 3" OUTSIDE THE MILWAUKIE
HISTORICAL MUSEUM

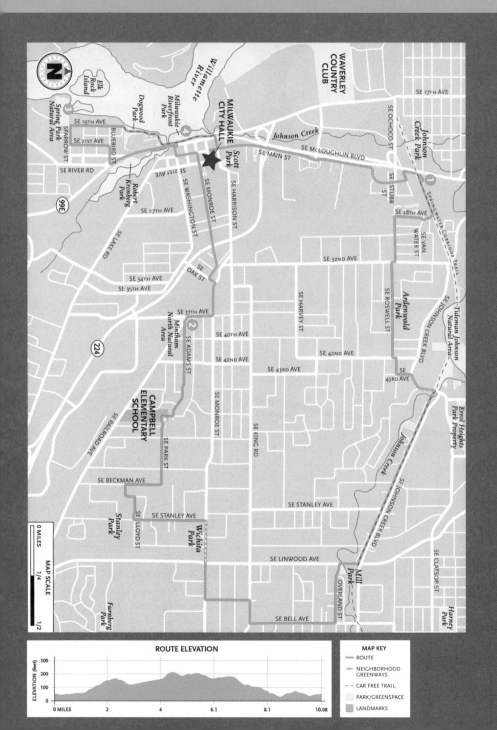

ROUTE ELEVATION

MAP KEY

ROUTE

NEIGHBORHOOD GREENWAYS

CAR FREE TRAIL

PARK/GREENSPACE

LANDMARKS

0.0 mi. Begin at the corner of SE Main and SE Jackson and ride along Main with City Hall on your right. The parking lot across from City Hall is home to the Milwaukie Sunday Farmer's Market, mid-May through October, named the region's best by the Oregonian in 2012. The contrast of buildings along Main is stark: the castle-like Milwaukie Masonic Lodge sits next door to brand new mixed-use apartments and retail space. Behind the Masonic Lodge is the Ledding Library and behind the library is Scott Park, home to a nice pond, lunchtime concerts in summer, and a colony of nutria, a South American rodent and beaver relative.

0.9 mi. As Main curves right, away from Highway 99E, look for a handsome granite building. It was built in 1938 as a New Deal jobs program and housed the regional headquarters for the Department of Transportation until 1995. Vacant ever since, the City of Milwaukie has been eyeing it for a museum, brewpub, or library. Why not all three? To get a closer look at its rough-hewn granite blocks and deep windowsills, turn left on SE Stubb and ride the short block to the dead end.

1.1 mi. Left on SE Moores and right onto the sidewalk of Highway 99E.

1.23 mi. Turn right on the path under the McLoughlin Bridge that leads onto the Springwater Corridor Trail and turn left, away from Highway 99E. Completed in 2006, the graceful arch of the 200-foot McLoughlin Bridge is the trail's signature span. It took almost 20 years to gather the $4.7 million to build this bridge and the two others needed to complete the trail from Sellwood to Boring.

1.51 mi. Right at the wooden signpost marked "SE 28th."

1.7 mi. Left on SE Roswell.

1.96 mi. At SE 32nd, turn right and then left to stay on Roswell. Pass by Ardenwald Park, where concerts (jazz, marimba, blues, and even polka) are held on Thursday evenings in August. Across the street at Ardenwald Elementary, kids and parents congregate every September to celebrate the new school year with the Ardenwald Bicycle Parade.

2.46 mi. At SE 42nd, turn left and then right to stay on Roswell.

2.56 mi. Left on SE 43rd and right on SE Johnson Creek.

2.81 mi. Turn right on the Springwater Corridor and cross Johnson Creek, which after much work by governmental agencies and activist groups, looks clean enough to splash in or at least enjoy its quiet gurgling and lush banks.

3.78 mi. Right on SE Linwood and left on SE Overland. Just after the turn is cute Mill Park. Its highlight is access to Johnson Creek, where kids hunt crawdads in the summer like in any other small Oregon town—the only difference is that we're in the middle of the state's largest metropolitan area.

4.2 mi. Right on semi-busy SE Bell.

4.7 mi. Right on busy SE King and left on SE 66th.

5.05 mi. Right on SE Monroe. After crossing Linnwood, Monroe suddenly becomes a neighborhood greenway with sharrows and bike signage.

5.5 mi. Left on SE Stanley.

5.8 mi. Right on SE Lloyd.

5.99 mi. Left on SE 56th. Go through the barricade on the short dirt path and continue on 56th.

6.1 mi. Turn right on SE Beckman Terrace (this becomes SE Park).

6.5 mi. At SE 48th, go straight on the tiny path between houses and turn right in the middle of the playground of the former Hector Campbell Elementary School, closed in 2012 because of budget cutbacks. The community garden within the playground rents out the majority of plots, but reserves four for volunteers to grow food for low-income families.

1 Here on the Springwater Corridor you're on the northern edge of both the City of Milwaukie and Clackamas County; Portland and Multnomah County are just to the left. The set of bulky, unassuming, beige industrial buildings is Precision Castparts, one of Oregon's two Fortune 500 companies. It makes cast metal pieces for aerospace (each Boeing 787 Dreamliner built earns the company $1.5 million), medical, oil and gas, defense, and automobile industries, and has plants and companies worldwide. Still, it's nowhere near as sexy as Nike. As you ride along the Springwater Corridor, you'll see a mishmash of other industrial and retail businesses, including the derelict-looking Hogan Steel Fabricators, Golden West Pool tables (poker tables too), and Wichita Feed and Hardware.

2 ——————

The Milwaukie Historical Museum (open on weekend afternoons) is in this poorly remodeled 1865 farmhouse. But you don't have to go inside to check out the star attraction: "Old No. 3," an original horse-drawn streetcar from 1872 once owned by the Portland Street Railway Co. Across the railroad tracks to the left is the Minthorn North Natural Area, a 6-acre wetland full of birds, beavers, and other wildlife. You can reach its oft-muddy trails for a stroll via a pathway on SE 37th.

6.71 mi. Left on SE Adams and enjoy the downhill ride.

7.21 mi. Right on SE Railroad and right on SE 37th. Pull over for a close up look at "Old No. 3" **2**.

7.3 mi. Left on SE Monroe.

7.37 mi. Left on SE Oak, right on SE Campbell and left on Monroe.

8.24 mi. Left on SE Main and right on SE Washington. On the corner of Main and Monroe sits the accurately named Main Street Collectors Mall and Soda Fountain.

8.36 mi. Cross McLoughlin and turn left on the Kellogg Creek Path (it begins at the far left corner of the parking lot). Ride through green Kellogg Park with its great river views, stands of trees, inviting picnic tables, and rocky beach. As you pass over the bridge above Kellogg Creek, notice the concrete fish ladder, with short jumps for spawning fish to get up from the Willamette to the higher reaches of the creek. Milwaukie's "other" creek was dammed to form Kellogg Lake in the 1890s. It was swimmable within living memory, but today sits at the bottom of the EPA's water-quality rankings. However, the city has plans to remove the dam and restore the creek with the goal of bringing back once-plentiful salmon runs, and human recreation.

8.76 mi. Follow the path as it merges with SE 19th.

9.05 mi. Where SE 19th ends at SE Sparrow is the Spring Park Natural Area **3**. Turn left on Sparrow, go under the train trestle, and turn left on SE 21st. On the right is the backside of the Milwaukie Grange Hall, a relic of the area's farming past.

3

The drawback to natural areas such as Spring Park is that dense vegetation and low traffic also attract people who have nowhere else to live, and without regular garbage service the results can be an eyesore. The local community has worked hard over the years to return Spring Park to its natural state and keep it nice and trash-free. A path leads to Elk Rock Island Park, the basalt remnant of a volcanic eruption 40 million years ago. The 13-acre island is accessible on foot only in late summer when the water levels are low enough, and its remote nature makes it a great place to view resident bald eagles, peregrine falcons, and waterfowl.

9.36 mi. Right on SE Bluebird. Cross SE 22nd and turn left on the Trolley Trail on the edge of SE McLoughlin. On your left, across McLoughlin, hidden in the grass is mistreated Kellogg Lake.

9.75 mi. The Trolley Trail brings you back to Milwaukie Riverfront Park **4** (after passing Kellogg Creek Water Pollution Control Plant and its less than wholesome smells).

9.97 mi. Right on SE Harrison and right on SE Main.

10.08 mi. Back to the start.

4

Milwaukie Riverfront Park sits in the middle of the outflow of Kellogg Creek, Johnson Creek, and the tranquil Willamette River. Called "Milwaukie's Living Room," the city is busily redecorating. Until the 1990s this was Milwaukie's working waterfront—marked by the remnants of lumber, grist, and shingle mills— and was the terminus of a ferry to the other side of the river until 1940. To the left is Klein Overlook with a great view of the picturesque final turn of Johnson Creek as it flows into the Willamette, hidden from all but those who go slow enough and close enough to enjoy it.

24 OAK GROVE AND THE TROLLEY TRAIL

STARTING POINT
SE McLoughlin Boulevard and SE Park Avenue

8.39 miles

DISTANCE

MODERATE
217 feet

DIFFICULTY & ELEVATION GAIN

SCAVENGER HUNT

Three mosaic-covered concrete cubes with images of the river, trolley, and local wildlife

....

A neon wiener dog

....

A pair of dragon-shaped driveway gates

....

A bench with a crow carved in it

TRANSIT AND PARKING

TriMet bus 33 stops at SE McLoughlin and SE Park, and as of 2015, TriMet's MAX Orange Line will serve the SE Park station at the same intersection. Look for street parking on SE 27th Pl and SE 27th Ave.

THE CONVERTED TROLLEY TRAIL has put Oak Grove—perhaps the biggest unincorporated city in Clackamas County—on the map, at least for bicyclists, walkers, and joggers. The original streetcar connected rural communities and made the world a little smaller. Redeveloping the trail makes the world, if not smaller, then slower and friendlier as joggers, walkers, dogs, and bicyclists greet one another on the path. Besides exploring much of the Trolley Trail, this ride takes you along River Road's pleasant bike lane before heading down to the river where ultra-quiet forested lanes, a hidden lake, and luxury homes await.

THE WILLAMETTE RIVER FROM A BOAT
RAMP IN OAK GROVE

The Trolley Trail was once a streetcar path that ran from Portland to Oregon City from 1893 until 1968. Since its closure, trail advocates lobbied to get the old line turned into a multi-use path, and in 2001 the right-of-way was purchased as a first step to make the dream come true. The 6-mile path opened in 2011, connecting the Springwater Corridor to the north with the I-205 path to the south, providing the missing link in an ever-growing system of car-free paths. Hooray!

Locals remember jumping off the trolley in the 1950s and going up McLoughlin to Roake's Hot Dogs (18109 SE McLoughlin) for a Coney Island dog and some flirting. If so inclined, you can do the same because Roake's is still serving burgers, onion rings, Coney dogs, and fries covered in their signature chili, the way they always have.

0.0 mi. Begin at the corner of SE McLoughlin and SE Park. Ride west on Park, uphill and away from McLoughlin. Turn left on the Trolley Trail ❶.

0.4 mi. Look for two cute stone cottages on your right, and almost directly across from them, a Clackamas County heritage tree with scaly bark and haunted house branches. The sign at the base of this imposing elder identifies it as an atlas cedar.

0.63 mi. The Trolley Trail merges with SE Arista at SE Courtney. Stay on Arista.

1.06 mi. At the intersection of Arista and SE Oak Grove you'll find the center of the Oak Grove community. With a small market, pub, sewing shop, and gift store, you could be in a tiny Oregon town instead of the middle of a city. If you're here on a Saturday, May through September, check out the Oak Grove Farmers Market. Continue on Arista.

1.33 mi. Turn left on the Trolley Trail across from 15215 SE Arista. This next section of trail is sandwiched between two streets running parallel to the tracks, with stately Craftsman homes set back from the road. Here you'll also begin to see signs for "River Forest Creek Watershed."

2.6 mi. Pass Stringfield Park on your right. The park was purchased by Metro funds from a natural areas bond measure and opened in 2011. The money has been used to restore sluggish Boardman Creek (which runs through the park), install the informative interpretive signs about the creek and surrounding wetlands, and build bike-friendly bridges over the waterway.

3.37 mi. The Trolley Trail dumps you out on SE McLoughlin where a trolley station once stood ❷. Turn right on McLoughlin and ride on the sidewalk for a block. Turn right on SE Jennings.

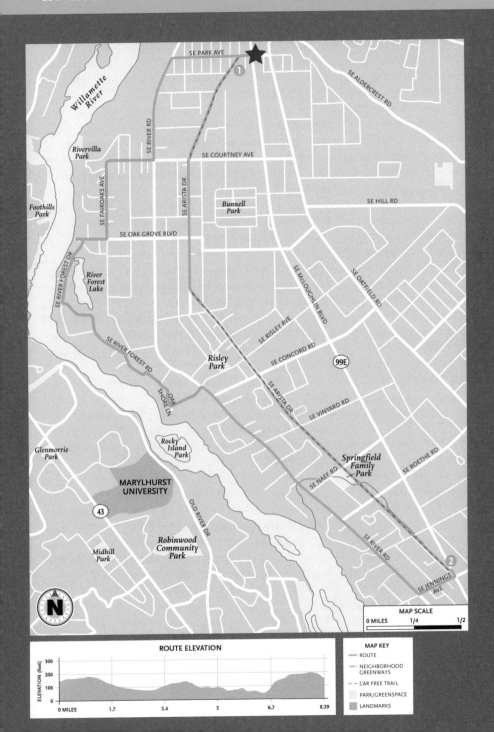

SE PARK AVE

Willamette River

Rivervilla Park

SE RIVER RD

Foothills Park

SE COURTNEY AVE

SE FAIROAKS AVE

SE ARISTA DR

Bunnell Park

SE HILL RD

SE ALDERCREST RD

SE OAK GROVE BLVD

SE RIVER FOREST DR

River Forest Lake

SE MCLOUGHLIN BLVD

SE OATFIELD RD

SE RIVER FOREST RD

Risley Park

SE RISLEY AVE

SE CONCORD RD

99E

OAK SHORE LN

SE ARISTA DR

SE VINYARD RD

Glenmorrie Park

Rocky Island Park

Springfield Family Park

SE ROETHE RD

SE NAEF RD

MARYLHURST UNIVERSITY

43

OLD RIVER DR

Robinwood Community Park

Midhill Park

SE RIVER RD

SE JENNINGS AVE

2

N

MAP SCALE

0 MILES   1/4   1/2

ROUTE ELEVATION

ELEVATION (feet)

300
200
100

0 MILES   1.7   3.4   5   6.7   8.39

MAP KEY

— ROUTE

NEIGHBORHOOD GREENWAYS

- - CAR FREE TRAIL

PARK/GREENSPACE

LANDMARKS

3.59 mi. Right on SE River. With its big firs and huge cedars alongside the 6-foot-wide bike lane, this is a much more enjoyable place to ride than Mcloughlin.

5.21 mi. Turn left on SE Risley and ride down the steep hill.

5.42 mi. Right on SE Oak Shore Lane. Holy giant edifices, there are some big ole' mansions down here! Where Oak Shore curves left and becomes SE River Forest Pl, you'll come upon Risley Landing Gardens, named for Orville Risley who settled this area in the early 1850s. The property remained in the family until it was donated to the Oak Grove Garden Club in 1983, but it's only open to groups by permission.

5.85 mi. Left on SE River Forest Rd. River Forest Lake on the right is where the watershed ends up. This idyllic little lake is enjoyed almost exclusively by those who live on its shores, but you can catch a glimpse of it at either end.

6.33 mi. At the T intersection, turn right on River Forest Dr.

6.68 mi. Left on SE Oak Grove. Follow the steep boat ramp down to the river. In the 1920s, before being developed into the estates you see today, this was Oak Grove Beach. Besides swimming, the area offered a dance pavilion, restaurant, and cottages. To the right is the 1910 Lake Oswego Railroad Bridge. Although it's never been used for anything more than freight rail, people have proposed allowing commuter rail, or bicycle and pedestrian traffic, across it.

Return back up Oak Grove. This is the big hill of the ride and a great candidate for walking if you don't have the appropriate gears, youthful legs, or lung capacity.

6.9 mi. Left on SE Fairoaks. If you've been looking for the oak trees in Oak Grove, here they are. Where Fairoaks turns right and becomes SE Courtney, you can see Rivervilla Park below.

7.59 mi. Left on SE River.

8.15 mi. Right on SE Park.

8.39 mi. Back to the start.

25 OREGON CITY TO GLADSTONE

THIS RIDE STARTS IN the middle of Oregon City, the oldest city west of the Rockies (founded in 1844), the first seat of state government, and the birthplace of Oregon industry. You'll explore the charming, revitalized main street and historic waterfront, see the roaring Willamette Falls, and roll through the new parks built to reconnect the people with their river and history. Then, you'll cross the rushing Clackamas River, see what the fishers are catching, and ramble through the river-side neighborhoods of unincorporated Clackamas County, before jumping on the Trolley Trail, a historic trolley line turned multi-use path, that leads into cute downtown Gladstone. After visiting this one-time farm and mill town, you'll see one of the most historic trees in the state—site of trials and weddings—ride along the wooded banks of the river, and re-cross the Clackamas to further meander through a forest, fields, and along a manmade lagoon before circling back to Oregon City.

SCAVENGER HUNT

A man-made waterfall

....

A sculpture of jumping fish made from logging cables and old oil tanks

....

STARTING POINT

Oregon City Transit Center (Main Street between Moss and 11th streets)

10.34 miles

DISTANCE

EASY 184 feet

DIFFICULTY & ELEVATION GAIN

A CAR-FREE BRIDGE OVER THE CLACKAMAS RIVER

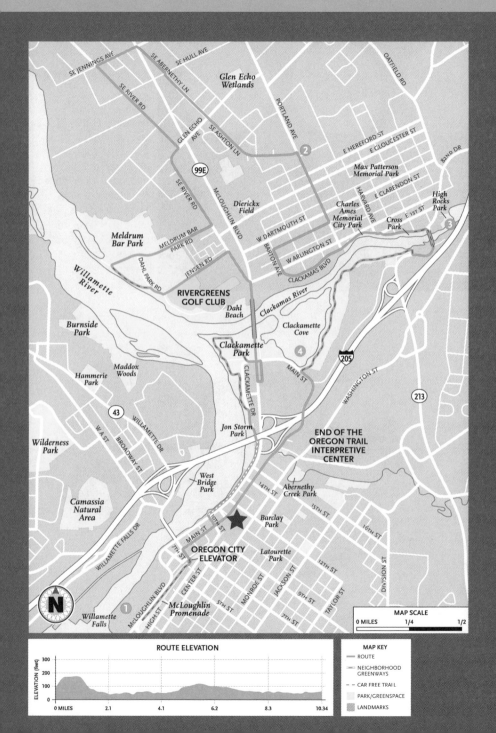

Glen Echo Wetlands

SE JENNINGS AVE
SE RIVER RD
SE ABERNETHY LN
SE HULL AVE
OATFIELD RD
PORTLAND AVE
GLEN ECHO AVE
SE ASHTON LN
99E
E HEREFORD ST
E GLOUCESTER ST
82ND DR
Max Patterson Memorial Park
SE RIVER RD
McLOUGHLIN BLVD
Dierickx Field
HARVARD AVE
E CLARENDON ST
High Rocks Park
Charles Ames Memorial City Park
Cross Park
E 1ST ST
2
Meldrum Bar Park
MELDRUM BAR PARK RD
W DARTMOUTH ST
BARTON AVE
3
Willamette River
DAHL PARK RD
JENSEN RD
W ARLINGTON ST
CLACKAMAS BLVD
RIVERGREENS GOLF CLUB
Dahl Beach
Clackamas River
Clackamette Cove
Burnside Park
Maddox Woods
Clackamette Park
4
205
Hammerie Park
CLACKAMETTE DR
MAIN ST
43
WILLAMETTE DR
Jon Storm Park
WASHINGTON ST
213
Wilderness Park
W A ST
BROADWAY ST
END OF THE OREGON TRAIL INTERPRETIVE CENTER
Camassia Natural Area
West Bridge Park
14TH ST
Abernethy Creek Park
15TH ST
16TH ST
WILLAMETTE FALLS DR
MAIN ST
16TH ST
Barclay Park
OREGON CITY ELEVATOR
7TH ST
Latourette Park
12TH ST
MONROE ST
JACKSON ST
9TH ST
TAYLOR ST
S DIVISION ST
N
McLOUGHLIN BLVD
HIGH ST
CENTER ST
5TH ST
7TH ST
1
Willamette Falls
McLoughlin Promenade

MAP SCALE
0 MILES   1/4   1/2

ROUTE ELEVATION

ELEVATION (feet)
300
200
100

0 MILES   2.1   4.1   6.2   8.3   10.34

MAP KEY
—— ROUTE
--- NEIGHBORHOOD GREENWAYS
-·- CAR FREE TRAIL
PARK/GREENSPACE
LANDMARKS

Horseshoe-shaped, 40-foot-high, 1500-foot-wide Willamette Falls is the second largest waterfall in the country by volume (it ranks 18th in the world). More importantly, the natural barrier to fish meant the falls provided Native Americans with food all winter. It also meant power for mills and a stopping point for boats wanting to use the river for transportation.

Dr. John McLoughlin built a sawmill on the falls in 1829, followed by two more, and the log camp quickly developed into a town. This made it the natural end to The Oregon Trail and within 25 years, hundreds of thousands of new settlers made this their destination before pursuing new lives in the Willamette Valley and beyond. The first paper mill was built in 1866 and locks were built around the falls in 1873. Oregon City maintained its position as the first city in the state until 1850 when Portland, with its deeper port, gained access to the rich fields of the valleys. In 1889 the falls provided the power to send the country's first long-distance power transmission to Portland, presaging Bonneville Dam several decades later.

Running right up to the falls, this massive ex–paper mill encompasses the original town site, and besides paper, was home to flour, wool, and brick mills, and a power plant. Ideas for redeveloping the site have included Pearl District–style mixed-use retail and apartments, a university, and a park. Time will tell what happens.

0.0 mi. Begin in Oregon City on Main Street between Moss and 11th; with your back to the river, turn right on Main. The vibrant downtown full of shops, restaurants, and history might tempt you to simply walk this first section.

At 10th, as you look up to the left, you can see the bluff rising above the city center. The white house up there is Dr. John McLoughlin's original home, moved from near the Willamette Falls up to the bluff in 1909 to save it from demolition. The McLoughlin House is open for visits from mid-February to mid-December.

0.25 mi. Turn left on 7th and ride one block to the intersection of Railroad Ave. Take the Oregon City Municipal Elevator to the top and turn right on the McLoughlin Promenade. The elevator connects lower downtown with the rest of the city, 130 feet up the cliff. This version with its great views of the Willamette Falls was built in 1952; the original (from 1915) was powered by water and took three minutes to get to the top. Today's elevator takes only 15 seconds and is operated by a city employee to prevent vandalism. The tunnel leading to the elevator, which runs under the Southern Pacific railroad tracks, has great photos of the old elevator and construction of the current one.

0.63 mi. Ride along the promenade (yield to pedestrians on the narrow path) to the last bench before the steep downhill where the promenade ends. Enjoy the unparalleled views of the region, the paper mills, and the Willamette Falls ❶ as they tumble down the rocky cliffs.

0.93 mi. Return the way you came on the promenade and down the elevator. From 7th, turn right on Main.

1.2 mi. Left on 10th. Cross Hwy 99E/McLoughlin to the river (go up on the sidewalk to trigger the crossing light) and turn right on the signed Willamette Greenway Trail. This wide, well-designed pathway was installed in 2008 to make the riverfront more attractive and accessible. Ride downriver on the trail, passing docks and kayak rentals.

1.73 mi. Turn left into Jon Storm Park, named for a volunteer killed while removing a tree from nearby Clackamette Park. In the shadow of the I-205 bridge, this park sits on the site of a former logging operation and features a cantilevered platform where you can feel the river's power as it surges under your feet in winter or meanders lazily in summer. Continue on the sidewalk along the river.

1.91 mi. Just before the Best Western hotel entrance, turn left on the bike path. This leads into Clackamette Park, a great spot to get close to the Willamette's final major tributary, the Clackamas River, as they merge.

2.1 mi. At the T intersection (at the RV park), turn left. Follow the path as it curves right and stays along the river.

2.32 mi. Turn right as the path ends at a road along the Clackamas. The confluence of the two rivers is just to your left. Turn right again just before the boat ramp.

The skateboard park on the left, just before leaving the park, seems to have more BMX bikes doing tricks in the concrete bowl than skateboards, including tiny tots just learning to ride but already eyeing the gnarly tailwhips and abubacas the big kids are pulling off.

2.54 mi. Left on Clackamette. Ride under the overpass and turn immediately right on the unmarked road.

2.69 mi. Turn right at the top of the hill and right again on McLoughlin. Ride on the sidewalk (the bike lane ends at the bridge) and cross the Clackamas River Bridge, built in 1932. If the Willamette is moving swiftly, then this river can only be described as raging.

Portland Avenue was once the dividing line between two donation land claims and named for the trolley that ran from here to the city of Portland. Oregon City attorney and one-time state senator Harvey Cross purchased enough of one of the claims to establish a town that in 1889 he named after his hero, four-time English Prime Minister William Ewart Gladstone. He named the east-west running streets after American universities and the north-south streets after English dukes and earls (Boston's Back Bay neighborhood shares the same street names).

3.17 mi. Turn left on SE River Road (cross W Arlington and cross SE McLoughlin using the pedestrian lights).

3.37 mi. Turn left on the path that leads around the fence on unmarked SE Jensen (after Taco Bell and before the Gladstone Mobile Home Park), entering the nearly 300-acre Meldrum Bar Park. The gentle downhill path opens up to baseball fields.

3.75 mi. Turn right as the path ends on unmarked Dahl Park Road (a park and boat ramp are to the left). Turn left on the unmarked path across from the Gladstone Gardening Association's vegetable gardens, and ride along the cliff above the Willamette and through the green mixed-deciduous forest.

4.06 mi. Turn right on unmarked Meldrum Bar Park Road. On the right behind the split rail fence is something you don't see every day: a radio-controlled car track, complete with dirt berms and little cars zipping all over the course.

4.59 mi. Left on SE River Rd. The name changes to SE Glen Echo as the road turns right.

5.01 mi. Left on SE River Rd.

5.57 mi. Right on SE Jennings Lodge.

5.79 mi. Cross SE McLoughlin and turn right onto the sidewalk and then immediately left after the electric substation on the Trolley Trail. Enjoy the relaxed, car-free riding along this rail-to-trail with classic old homes on both sides.

6.79 mi. Turn right where the trail ends at a sidewalk on Portland Ave , which leads to downtown Gladstone. Downtown doesn't get much more compact than this: pass the post office, volunteer fire department, police station, and City Hall in a few blocks, followed by taverns, a cafe, and a market. The Flying A Service station—a lovingly restored art deco gas station (now an ATV accessories shop) with period tin signs, gas pumps, and an old pickup out front—complete the "small town lost in time" theme.

7.14 mi. Right on W Clarendon.

7.43 mi. Turn left on Barton which becomes W Clackamas. Across from 235 W Clackamas is the gnarled, half dead, half-green Pow-Wow tree. More than 200 years old, the Pow-Wow tree is Gladstone's city emblem. This big leaf maple was once an outdoor courthouse and meeting place for the Clackamas and Multnomah Native American tribes, and has been the site of countless compacts, weddings, and celebrations, as well as the first county and state fairs in 1860 and 1861.

7.93 mi. W Clackamas gives way to a path through Charles Ames Park and then Cross Park, where you'll find nice views through the woods of the swift running river below. There's a steep access path down to the river and a relaxing picnic area halfway down.

8.33 mi. Exit Cross Park (a side trip to view High Rocks Park is an option here) and turn right at the round-about to cross the car-free bridge over the river. This bridge carried automobiles from 1921 until 1986 when it became bike and pedestrian only. Don't you just love a car-free bridge over a river?

3

To view one of Oregon's notoriously dangerous swimming spots, turn left on SE 82nd Dr after exiting Cross Park. From 82nd, turn right just after the office build-ing at 25 82nd Ave and head down the short road to High Rocks Park. This infamous swimming hole, although impres-sive to look at with its rock cliffs and swift flow-ing river, claims swim-mers' lives every year, as the sign in the park-ing lot sternly warns. In summer, lifeguards in red trunks work to keep swimmers safe.

4

Clackamette Cove was originally a wetland, but decades of sand and gravel mining created first a lake and finally the cove. Asphalt and concrete were also produced here, and at some point a large amount of gasoline was spilled. Besides gasoline and asphalt, the ground here contains heavy metals, diesel, lube oil, and chlorinated hydrocarbons. Nasty.

When an illegal BMX track was discovered here in 2011, a big hubbub ensued including action by the city to dismantle and remediate its environmental damage. One of the outlaw builders of the track came forward and said that while his crew of shovel-wielding berm-builders had rearranged the natural landforms, the damage they did paled in comparison with previous outrages. Meanwhile, a project to bring hundreds of apartments and condos, offices, a park, and an amphitheater to the shores of Clackamette Cove has been in negotiations between the city and developers since 2006.

8.55 mi. Turn right at the end of the bridge and right again on the Clackamas River Trail (follow the bike sign "Dntwn Oregon City"). This lovely trail runs along the south bank of the Clackamas, through a deciduous forest of cottonwood and big leaf maple, past the same de-commissioned bridge you passed on the other side of the river, and through an old landfill and quarry, Clackamette Cove **4**.

9.47 mi. Left on unmarked Main where the path ends (again marked "Dntwn Oregon City"). After you go under I-205, you'll see the giant frames of three Conestoga Wagons that signals the End of the Oregon Trail Interpretive Center. This struggling museum recounts the lives of the 300,000 pioneers who came here looking for opportunity and up to 640 acres of free land.

10.34 mi. Back to the start.

BIKE RENTAL AND REPAIR

BIKE COMMUTER
pdxbikecommuter.com
8315 SE 13th Ave
503-505-9200

THE BIKE GALLERY
bikegallery.com
Downtown: 1001 SW Salmon
503-222-3821
Hollywood: 5329 NE Sandy Blvd
503-281-9800

CLEVER CYCLES
clevercycles.com
908 SE Hawthorne Boulevard
503-334-1560

CYCLE PORTLAND BICYCLE TOURS
portlandbicycletours.com
117 NW 2nd Ave
503-902-5035

EVERYBODY'S BIKE RENTALS
pdxbikerentals.com
NE 19th and Alberta (by appointment)
503-893-4519

FAT TIRE FARM
fattirefarm.com
2714 NW Thurman
503-222-3276

GO BY BIKE SHOP
gobybikepdx.com
SW Moody and Gibbs
971-271-9270

HOLLYWOOD CYCLING
hollywoodcycling.net
5258 NE Sandy Blvd
503-281-1671

KALKHOFF ELECTRIC BICYCLES
www.kalkhoffusa.com
528 NW 11th Ave
503-220-2300

**KERR BIKES /
WHEEL FUN RENTALS**
www.albertinakerr.org/KerrBikes/
Overview.aspx
1020 SW Naito Parkway
503-808-9955

PEDAL BIKE TOURS
pedalbiketours.com
133 SW 2nd Ave
503-243-2453

SELLWOOD CYCLE REPAIR
sellwoodcycle.com
7639 SE Milwaukie
503-233-9392

SPLENDID CYCLES
splendidcycles.com
1407 SE Belmont
503-954-2620

VELOCE BICYCLES
velocebicycles.com
3202 SE Hawthorne
503-234-8400

WATERFRONT BICYCLE RENTALS
waterfrontbikes.com
10 SW Ash Street, #100
503-227-1719

WESTERN BIKE WORKS
westernbikeworks.com
1015 NW 17th Ave
503-342-9985

SCAVENGER HUNT ANSWER KEY

RIDE 1
Railroad track fence: Tanner Springs Park
Zoobomb pile: W Burnside Street and SE 13th Avenue
Teddy Roosevelt statue: South Park Blocks

RIDE 2
Willamette River model: Eastbank Esplanade by the Hawthorne Bridge
Statues of snails: The Fields Neighborhood Park
Pair of tall stainless steel sculptures: Governor Tom McCall Waterfront Park, between the Steel Bridge and the cherry trees

RIDE 3
Topiary animals: Rose Garden Children's Park
Sacajawea Statue: Washington Park, SW Lewis Clark Way
Pedal garden: NW 13th and NW Johnson

RIDE 4
"Peggy" the train: World Forestry Center

Donkeys: Front yard of 83220 SW Canyon Drive
Log fort: SW Kennedy & SW 103rd

RIDE 5
Roadside library: 11865 SW 95th
Big tree stump: Camille Park
Beetle chimney: On SW Florence outside Florence Pointe Park

RIDE 6
Six duck ponds: Waterhouse South Powerline Park, near Estuary Dr. (1); Willow Creek Greenway (2); Waterhouse Lake (3); HM Terpenning Recreation Complex, Waterhouse Creek (4 and 5); and Commonwealth Lake (6).
Castle house: 888 NW 170th
Fire truck–shaped bike rack: Wanda Peck Memorial Park

RIDE 7
Fountain with jets: 53rd Avenue Community park
Octagonal barn: Cornelius Pass Roadhouse
Sandstone rock: Orchard Park playground

RIDE 8

Bronze statues: Beverly Cleary Statue Garden, Grant Park
Dolphin weathervane: 3365 NE Alameda
Stethoscope bike rack: NE 42nd and NE Broadway

RIDE 9

Pavement murals: NE Going and NE 6th, NE 13th and NE Webster, and NE 8th and NE Holman
Lego head posts: Holman City Park
"Green" bike rack, green roof: Breakside Brewery, 820 NE Dekum

RIDE 10

Tombstone and tree: Lone Fir Cemetery, just past the columnar incense cedar
Cuban mural: Pambiche, 2811 NE Glisan
Poetry post and art tree: 2523 NE 25th

RIDE 11

A fence whose bars has metal images of dogs: Glenhaven Dog Park, Banfield Pet Hospital, NE 82nd and NE Tillamook
Colorful pavement mural: NE 77th and NE Beech
Park in the street: Roseway Parkway
George Washington statue: NE Sandy, NE Alameda & NE 57th

RIDE 12

Intersection mural: N Overlook and N Failing

"M" state streets: Massachusetts (only crossed at the beginning of the tour), Maryland, Montana, Missouri, Michigan, and Mississippi
Two bronze sea turtles: Harper's Playground, Arbor Lodge Park

RIDE 13

Whirlymajig: front courtyard of the Charles Jordan Community Center
Tree street painting: N Sedro and N Gilbert

RIDE 14

Beaver skull sculpture: N Marine, Smith and Bybee Wetlands
River confluence: Kelley Point Park

RIDE 15

Beaver Totem Pole: Clark College campus
Statue of girl with flower: Esther Short Park

RIDE 16

Submarine: Oregon Museum of Science & Industry
Bird mural: bluff above Oaks Bottom Wildlife Refuge

RIDE 17

Two bikes mounted on poles: SE Clinton between SE 29th and 30th, and at SE 34th
Smiling chimney: NE 41st and NE Burnside

Winged monster: On top of City-bikes, 1914 SE Ankeny.

RIDE 18

Nike regrind court: Ed Benedict Park
Monkey puzzle tree: 14619 SE Bush
A bike hanging over a garage door: 6515 SE 94th

RIDE 19

Metal gate with Chinese characters: SE 85th and SE Clinton
Benjamin Franklin statue: Franklin High
Golden geese weathervane: 101 SE 54th

RIDE 20

Gold Buddha: Kwan Yin Temple, 16525 Northeast Glisan
Turtle rock: Nadaka Nature Park, NE 175th and NE Pacific
Motorcycle sculpture: 5250 SE Circle

RIDE 21

Colorful tiles of plants and animals: front steps of Woodstock Elementary
Round tower with a rooster weathervane: SE 51st and SE Gladstone
Pig weathervane: 5317 SE Center

RIDE 22

Reed Canyon Lake
Ferris wheel: Oaks Bottom Amusement Park

RIDE 23

Alien mannequins: Dark Horse Comics, SE Main and SE Jackson
American flag roof and bald eagle mural: Smith Rock Inc., 6001 SE Johnson Creek Blvd (off the Springwater Corridor)
Horse-drawn streetcar: Milwaukie History Museum

RIDE 24

Mosaic-covered concrete cubes: Riverside Elementary, SE Concord and the Trolley Trail
Neon wiener dog: Roake's Hot Dogs 18109 SE McLoughlin
A pair of dragon-shaped driveway gates: 1218 River Forest Road
Bench with crow: SE Fairoaks and SE Overlook Lane

RIDE 25

Man-made waterfall: Singer Creek Falls, 8th and Railroad Avenue
Jumping fish sculpture: Clackamette Park

ACKNOWLEDGMENTS

I'd like to thank some of the people who helped out with this book. First to my adventurous, level-headed, and down-to-earth wife, Lota, and unwitting daughter Serenne Coral Lamontagne-Roll. The former, who put up with my anxiety, indecision, impatience, and lamentations over many a month, and the latter, who was forced to vie for attention from her stressed-out father despite her inability to talk (but who has the unbeatable weapons of squeals, coos, and gurgles, in addition to being unbearably cute).

Thanks to Jason Brown, Crystal Eppinger, Sam Haffner, Sam Hagan, Amy Johnson, Brad Parker, Hayden Thompson, and Adriel Weiner for riding my maniacal routes and giving me their invaluable criticisms, especially where future unwitting riders might have perished without it.

Of course thanks to my editor, Mollie Firestone, who is hip, clever, and informed enough to bring me back from the brink of many routing and phrasing disasters and who is largely responsible for the most interesting aspects of this book.

Also deepest thanks to Laura Foster, whose books *Portland City Walks* and *Portland Hill Walks* are partially the inspiration and model for this book, whose edits were valuable, and who came up with the idea for the Scavenger Hunts. Many a biker nerd's children will thank you for it.

INDEX

ABOUT THE AUTHOR

An Oregon native, Todd Roll's adventures in Europe opened his eyes to biking as more than a sport for speed junkies in Lycra. His desire to make biking accessible to all spawned his Portland sightseeing company, Pedal Bike Tours, as well as the business motto "no spandex is required." Through Pedal Bike Tours, he has helped get thousands of tourists and locals onto bikes to pedal the most bike-friendly large city in America. Todd can be seen riding Pee Wee Herman 2 around Portland with his wife and daughter.

ERIN BERZEL PHOTOGRAPHY